First World War
and Army of Occupation
War Diary
France, Belgium and Germany

14 DIVISION
42 Infantry Brigade,
Brigade Machine Gun Company
1 March 1916 - 28 February 1918

WO95/1902/3

The Naval & Military Press Ltd
www.nmarchive.com
Published in association with The National Archives

Published by

The Naval & Military Press Ltd

Unit 10 Ridgewood Industrial Park,

Uckfield, East Sussex,

TN22 5QE England

Tel: +44 (0) 1825 749494

www.naval-military-press.com

www.nmarchive.com

This diary has been reprinted in facsimile from the original. Any imperfections are inevitably reproduced and the quality may fall short of modern type and cartographic standards.

© **Crown Copyright**
Images reproduced by permission of The National Archives, London, England, 2015.

Contents

Document type	Place/Title	Date From	Date To
Heading	14th Division 42nd Infy Bde 42nd Machine Gun Coy. Mar 1916-Feb 1918		
Heading	War Diary Of 42nd Brigade Machine Gun Company From March 1st To March 31st 1916		
War Diary	Simencourt	01/03/1916	04/03/1916
War Diary	Simencourt Arras	05/03/1916	05/03/1916
War Diary	Arras	06/03/1916	31/03/1916
Heading	War Diary Of 42nd Brigade Machine Gun Company For April 1916		
War Diary	Arras	22/04/1916	30/04/1916
War Diary	Arras	01/04/1916	21/04/1916
Heading	War Diary May 1916 42nd Brigade Machine Gun Coy.		
War Diary	Arras	01/05/1916	30/06/1916
Heading	War Diary 42nd Machine Gun Company 1st-31st July 1916		
War Diary	Arras	01/07/1916	27/07/1916
War Diary	Duisans & G de Rollecourt	28/07/1916	28/07/1916
War Diary	Gde Rullecourt-Mezerolles	29/07/1916	29/07/1916
War Diary	Mezerolles	30/07/1916	30/07/1916
War Diary	Mezerolles Fienvillers	31/07/1916	31/07/1916
Heading	42nd Brigade 14th Division. 42nd Brigade Machine Gun Company August 1916		
Heading	War Diary 42nd Machine Gun Coy Vol VI August 1916		
War Diary	Fienvillers	01/08/1916	07/08/1916
War Diary	Buire-Sur-L'Ancre	08/08/1916	11/08/1916
War Diary	Divisional Reserve Near Fricourt	12/08/1916	12/08/1916
War Diary	Near Fricourt	13/08/1916	18/08/1916
War Diary	Montauban And Trenches In Near Delville Wood	19/08/1916	24/08/1916
War Diary	Trenches in Delville Wood	24/08/1916	24/08/1916
War Diary	Delville Wood	25/08/1916	25/08/1916
War Diary	Bivouacs Near Fricourt	25/08/1916	25/08/1916
War Diary	Near Fricourt	26/08/1916	28/08/1916
War Diary	Dernancourt	30/08/1916	30/08/1916
War Diary	Dernancourt Avesnes	31/08/1916	31/08/1916
Heading	War Diary 42nd Machine Gun Company For September 1916 Volume VII		
War Diary	Agny G. Sector	27/09/1916	29/09/1916
War Diary	G. Sector	30/09/1916	30/09/1916
War Diary	Dernancourt	19/09/1916	21/09/1916
War Diary	Dernancourt Grand Bullecourt	22/09/1916	22/09/1916
War Diary	Grand Bullecourt	23/09/1916	23/09/1916
War Diary	Grand Bullecourt Berneville	24/09/1916	24/09/1916
War Diary	G. Sector (Agny)	25/09/1916	26/09/1916
War Diary	Near Fricourt	13/09/1916	13/09/1916
War Diary	Fricourt Montauban	14/09/1916	15/09/1916
War Diary	Montauban	16/09/1916	16/09/1916
War Diary	Near Fricourt	17/09/1916	17/09/1916
War Diary	Near Dernancourt	18/09/1916	18/09/1916
War Diary	Avesnes	01/09/1916	10/09/1916

War Diary	Avesnes Dernancourt	11/09/1916	11/09/1916
War Diary	Near Fricourt	12/09/1916	12/09/1916
Heading	War Diary 42nd Machine Gun Company Vol VIII. Oct. 1916		
War Diary	G Sector Agny	01/10/1916	26/10/1916
War Diary	Wanquetin	27/10/1916	27/10/1916
War Diary	Liencourt	28/10/1916	31/10/1916
Heading	War Diary Of 42nd Machine Gun Company. From 1st Novr 1916 To 30th Novr 1916 (Volume 9)		
War Diary	Liencourt	01/11/1916	22/11/1916
War Diary	Liencourt Gouyen Artois	23/11/1916	23/11/1916
War Diary	Gouyen Artois	24/11/1916	30/11/1916
Heading	War Diary 42nd Machine Gun Company From Dec 1st 1916 To Dec 31st 1916 Volume 10		
War Diary	Gouyen Artois	01/12/1916	07/12/1916
War Diary	Gouyen Artois Lignereuil	08/12/1916	08/12/1916
War Diary	Lignereuil	09/12/1916	09/12/1916
War Diary	Agny (G Sector) Vi Corps Front	16/12/1916	31/12/1916
Heading	War Diary 42nd Machine Gun Company. From 1st Jan 1917 To 31st Jan 1917		
War Diary	G. Sector VI Corps	01/01/1917	15/01/1917
War Diary	G. Sector VII Corps Front	16/01/1917	31/01/1917
Heading	War Diary 42nd Machine Gun Company From 1-2-17 To 28.2.17 Vol No XII		
War Diary	G Sector 7th Corps Front	01/02/1917	10/02/1917
War Diary	A. Sector VII Corps Front	11/02/1917	28/02/1917
Heading	War Diary 42nd Machine Gun Coy From 1-3-1917 To 31-3-1917 Volume 13		
War Diary	H Sector VII Corps Front	01/03/1917	07/03/1917
War Diary	G Sector VII Corps Front	08/03/1917	15/03/1917
War Diary	H Sector VII Corps Front	16/03/1917	24/03/1917
War Diary	Berneville	25/03/1917	31/03/1917
Heading	War Diary 42nd Machine Gun Company Vol. XIV April 1917		
War Diary	Berneville	01/04/1917	05/04/1917
War Diary	H Sector	06/04/1917	09/04/1917
War Diary	H Sector & Trenches Captured	09/04/1917	11/04/1917
War Diary	on the March	12/04/1917	12/04/1917
War Diary	Liencourt	14/04/1917	14/04/1917
War Diary	Le. Cauroy.	15/04/1917	22/04/1917
War Diary	Barly	23/04/1917	23/04/1917
War Diary	Bellacourt Old German Front Line	24/04/1917	24/04/1917
War Diary	Near Wancourt	25/04/1917	29/04/1917
War Diary	Trenches Near Wancourt	30/04/1917	30/04/1917
Heading	War Diary 42nd Machine Gun Company 1st-31st May. 1917 Vol. 15		
War Diary	Trenches Near Wancourt	01/05/1917	04/05/1917
War Diary	The Harp	05/05/1917	15/05/1917
War Diary	Support Area	16/05/1917	23/05/1917
War Diary	Trenches Left of VII Corps Front	24/05/1917	31/05/1917
Heading	War Diary 42nd Machine Gun Company Vol. XVI June 1917		
War Diary	Trenches Left Of VII Corps Front	01/06/1917	03/06/1917
War Diary	Beaurains	04/06/1917	08/06/1917
War Diary	Beaumetz	09/06/1917	09/06/1917
War Diary	Saulty	10/06/1917	10/06/1917

War Diary	Beauquesne	11/06/1917	30/06/1917
Heading	War Diary 42nd Machine Gun Coy. 1st To 31st July 1917 Vol 17		
War Diary	Beauquesne	01/07/1917	11/07/1917
War Diary	Bailleul	12/07/1917	31/07/1917
Heading	War Diary 42nd Machine Gun Company Volume XVIII August 1917		
War Diary	Bailleul	01/08/1917	06/08/1917
War Diary	Pradelles	07/08/1917	15/08/1917
War Diary	Oudedom	16/08/1917	17/08/1917
War Diary	Dikebusch	18/08/1917	18/08/1917
War Diary	Trenches Before Glencorse Wood	19/08/1917	26/08/1917
War Diary	Wippenhoek Area	27/08/1917	29/08/1917
War Diary	Thiushook Area	30/08/1917	31/08/1917
Heading	War Diary 42nd Machine Gun Company Volume XIX September 1917		
War Diary	Neuve Eglise Area	01/09/1917	02/09/1917
War Diary	Trenches East Of Messines	03/09/1917	12/09/1917
War Diary	Neuve Eglise Area	13/09/1917	15/09/1917
War Diary	Berquin Area	16/09/1917	18/09/1917
War Diary	Neuve Eglise Area	19/09/1917	30/09/1917
Heading	War Diary 42nd Machine Gun Company October 1917 Volume XX		
War Diary	Trenches East Of Messines	01/10/1917	08/10/1917
War Diary	Neuve Eglise	09/10/1917	10/10/1917
War Diary	Thieushook	11/10/1917	11/10/1917
War Diary	Ridge Wood	12/10/1917	16/10/1917
War Diary	Trenches West Of Polderhoek Chateau	17/10/1917	24/10/1917
War Diary	Thieushook	25/10/1917	31/10/1917
Heading	War Diary 42nd Machine Gun Coy. 1st To 30th November 1917 Volume No. 21		
War Diary	Thieushouk	01/11/1917	12/11/1917
War Diary	Westbecourt	13/11/1917	30/11/1917
Heading	War Diary 42nd Machine Gun Coy December 1917 Volume 22		
War Diary	Brandhoek	01/12/1917	03/12/1917
War Diary	Trenches	04/12/1917	09/12/1917
War Diary	St Jean	10/12/1917	14/12/1917
War Diary	Trenches	15/12/1917	21/12/1917
War Diary	Brandhoek	22/12/1917	25/12/1917
War Diary	Tatinghem	26/12/1917	31/12/1917
Heading	War Diary 42nd Machine Gun Coy. January 1918. Volume 23		
War Diary	Tatinghem	01/01/1918	01/01/1918
War Diary	Suzanne	02/01/1918	21/01/1918
War Diary	Vrely	22/01/1918	22/01/1918
War Diary	Saulchoy	23/01/1918	24/01/1918
War Diary	Beines	25/01/1918	25/01/1918
War Diary	Montescourt	26/01/1918	27/01/1918
War Diary	Trenches About 6 Miles South Of St Quentin	28/01/1918	31/01/1918
Heading	War Diary 42nd Machine Gun Company February 1918 Volume 24		
War Diary	Trenches	01/02/1918	28/02/1918

14TH DIVISION
42ND INFY BDE

42ND MACHINE GUN COY.

MAR 1916 - FEB 1918

CONFIDENTIAL

War Diary of
42nd Brigade Machine Gun Company

from March 1st
to   March 31st } 1916

Vol: 1

Army Form C. 2118.

WAR DIARY
or
INTELLIGENCE SUMMARY

(Erase heading not required.)

42nd Inf./Bde. Machine Gun Company

Instructions regarding War Diaries and Intelligence Summaries are contained in F. S. Regs., Part II. and the Staff Manual respectively. Title Pages will be prepared in manuscript.

Place	Date	Hour	Summary of Events and Information	Remarks and references to Appendices
SIMENCOURT	1/3/16		Company arrived from SOMBRIN to SIMENCOURT 8½ miles and took over billets from French troops.	
SIMENCOURT	2/3/16		Training continued after interval of several days owing to movement. Officers and four privates joined from Machine Gun Corps depot, near Aire La Q Les very little having previous to leaving England.	
SIMENCOURT	3/3/16		Training continued. Special class of instruction started for untrained officers and newly joined draft.	
SIMENCOURT	4/3/16		Training continued. Preliminary arrangements for taking over gun positions from 41st and 43rd Inf./Bde. Machine Gun Companies in trenches round ARRAS.	
SIMENCOURT – ARRAS.	5/3/16.		Company marched to ARRAS to billets preparatory to putting guns into the line. One officer class under sergeant instructor, transport and details left with one gun at transport camp SIMENCOURT.	
ARRAS.	6/3/16.		Four guns relieved four guns of 41st Inf/Bde. M.G.Coy. in positions in rear of front line by day; positions selected around RONVILLE. These guns relieved machine guns	

Army Form C. 2118.

WAR DIARY
or
INTELLIGENCE SUMMARY   49th Inf/Bde Machine Gun Company
(Erase heading not required.)

Instructions regarding War Diaries and Intelligence Summaries are contained in F.S. Regs., Part II. and the Staff Manual respectively. Title Pages will be prepared in manuscript.

Place	Date	Hour	Summary of Events and Information	Remarks and references to Appendices
ARRAS	6/3/16 (continued)		of 7 & 8 2nd Inf/Bde R.g. Coy in positions in rear of front line; positions selected East of ACHICOURT. Both reliefs carried out without incident. Billets changed.	
ARRAS	7/3/16		Nothing to report.	
ARRAS	8/3/16		Nothing to report.	
ARRAS	9/3/16		Defences of BONVILLE, ACHICOURT and ARRAS* reconnoitred with a view to their protection by machine guns. The country is admirably suited to machine guns and to obtain best results expert tunnelling labour is required.	*1st Line between ARRAS Railway Station and steel bridge on ARRAS - ACHICOURT Road.
ARRAS	10/3/16		Machine gun positions inspected by Brig. Gen. Cay 49 2nd Inf/Bde. Plan made of wire entanglements and certain emplacements which it is intended to make into strong posts with small garrisons consisting of the machine gun teams and a few extra men to hold out as long as possible in the event of the line being forced back.	
ARRAS	11/3/16		An instructor from Machine gun School G.H.Q. visited some of the gun positions.	

Army Form C. 2118.

WAR DIARY
or
INTELLIGENCE SUMMARY   42nd Inf/Bde Machine Gun Company
(Erase heading not required.)

Instructions regarding War Diaries and Intelligence Summaries are contained in F. S. Regs, Part II. and the Staff Manual respectively. Title Pages will be prepared in manuscript.

Place	Date	Hour	Summary of Events and Information	Remarks and references to Appendices
ARRAS	12/3/16		Whole Brigade Line reconnoitred for possible alterations and additions to machine gun positions	
ARRAS	13/3/16		Gas alarm 1.30am. "Stand to" ordered. Alarm proved false and "stand to" cancelled 2.45am.	
ARRAS	14/3/16		Orders received from Brig. Gen. Comg. 42nd Inf/Bde for two machine guns to be put into positions in front line as "stiffening" to trench guns. Two suitable positions found covering a large extent of the lines with flanking fire.	
ARRAS	14/3/16		Two guns put in position in previously erected emplacements at ARRAS and RONVILLE RAILWAY BRIDGE. Three guns relieved without incident.	
ARRAS	15/3/16		Nothing to report.	
ARRAS	16/3/16		Plans made of cathedral & new emplacement at ARRAS & covering 1st Line of ARRAS defences. Guns placed in temporary positions pending erection of splinter proofs. Four guns relieved without incident.	

Army Form C. 2118.

WAR DIARY
or
INTELLIGENCE SUMMARY

(Erase heading not required.)

H.Q. 2nd Inf/Bde Machine Gun Company

Instructions regarding War Diaries and Intelligence Summaries are contained in F.S. Regs., Part II. and the Staff Manual respectively. Title Pages will be prepared in manuscript.

Place	Date	Hour	Summary of Events and Information	Remarks and references to Appendices
ARRAS	17/3/16.		Co-operation between Machine Guns and Trench guns in left sector of Brigade front arranged between OC 6th KSLI and OC 2nd Bde M.G. Coy.	
ARRAS	18/3/16.		Heavy shelling of front and support line trenches by enemy. Two guns put into hastily improvised emplacements in H.B. line in case of infantry attack by enemy during night after bombardment.	
ARRAS	19/3/16.		ACHICOURT defences reconnoitred with a view to defence by Machine guns. Retaliation by our Artillery for previous days shelling orders received to open a few bursts of rapid fire into enemy's trenches in evening. This carried by Artillery retaliation. All arrangements made and gun stand direct at Lieut L. Wallis cancelled before fire was opened owing to arrival of cost assumed to be ARR by one or troops or trenches damaged by previous day's bombardment. Nothing to report.	
ARRAS	20/3/16.			
ARRAS	21/3/16.		Guns withdrawn from temporary emplacements occupied in H.B. line on 18th	

2449 Wt. W14957/M90 750,000 1/16 J.B.C. & A. Forms/C.2118/12.

Army Form C. 2118.

WAR DIARY
or
INTELLIGENCE SUMMARY

42nd Inf/Bde Machine Gun Coy.

(Erase heading not required.)

Instructions regarding War Diaries and Intelligence Summaries are contained in F.S. Regs., Part II. and the Staff Manual respectively. Title Pages will be prepared in manuscript.

Place	Date	Hour	Summary of Events and Information	Remarks and references to Appendices
ARRAS	21/3/16 continued		RONVILLE Defences reconnoitred with a view to putting two machine guns in to M.G. position.	
ARRAS	22/3/16		H-B line reconnoitred in conjunction with R.E. Officer; site for gun position flanking left of H-B line decided on in CHATEAU d'RONVILLE	
ARRAS	23/3/16		Nothing to report.	
ARRAS	24/3/16		Two possible positions found for guns to cover A.3 and H.B. lines.	
ARRAS	25/3/16		Co-operation between Vickers and Lewis Guns arranged with O.C. 5th Oxf & Bucks 28 Coy in left sector of Brigade Front. Sfus relieved without incident.	
ARRAS	26/3/16		Co-operation between Machine and Lewis guns arranged with O.C. 9th Rifle Brigade in right sector of Brigade Front. These guns relieved without incident.	
ARRAS	27/3/16		Nothing to report.	

Army Form C. 2118.

WAR DIARY
or
INTELLIGENCE SUMMARY

42nd Inf/Bde Machine Gun Company

(Erase heading not required.)

Instructions regarding War Diaries and Intelligence Summaries are contained in F.S. Regs., Part II. and the Staff Manual respectively. Title Pages will be prepared in manuscript.

Place	Date	Hour	Summary of Events and Information	Remarks and references to Appendices
ARRAS	28/3/16		Firing platforms built in new position in SCIERIE yard completed by R.E.	
ARRAS	29/3/16		Experiments carried out at miniature range with fixed angle pivoting mounting (Sergt Topfield pattern) and zenkin hyposcope. Both efficacy Satisfactory.	
ARRAS	30/3/16		Nothing to report.	
ARRAS	31/3/16		Nothing to report.	

G.F. Plunden Capt.
Comdg 42nd Inf/Bde M.G.Cy.

42 MG Coy Vol 2

XIV

War Diary

of

42ⁿᵈ Brigade Machine Gun Company

for

April 1916

Army Form C. 2118.

WAR DIARY
or
INTELLIGENCE SUMMARY

42nd Inf. Bde. Machine Gun Company

(Erase heading not required.)

Instructions regarding War Diaries and Intelligence Summaries are contained in F.S. Regs., Part II. and the Staff Manual respectively. Title Pages will be prepared in manuscript.

Place	Date	Hour	Summary of Events and Information	Remarks and references to Appendices
ARRAS	22/4/16		#35 – 26 sucenaded during bombardment by heavy artillery of enemy's lines, trenches covered by machine guns	
ARRAS	23/4/16		Nothing to report.	
ARRAS	24/4/16		Considerable artillery activity. #35 damaged, Lewis guns moved up the MG Sec to cover #35 in case of raid by enemy. One Officer proceeded on leave to U.K.	
ARRAS	25/4/16		Lewis guns, ordered up from Hqrs on the previous day were withdrawn	
ARRAS	26/4/16		Nothing to report.	
ARRAS	27/4/16		Relief of MG Guns carried out without incident on night April 26/27th. #33 – 35 evacuated during bombardment of enemy salient by Trench Mortars. Evacuated trenches covered by Machine Guns.	
ARRAS	28/4/16		Nothing to Report	
ARRAS	29/4/16		French party dug to Scienne Position. Platform started at Chateau Position.	
ARRAS	30/4/16		Platforms built at 2 positions.	

G.F. Pleisher Cpl.
Cmdg 42nd Inf/Bde M.G. Coy.

WAR DIARY or INTELLIGENCE SUMMARY

Army Form C. 2118.

HQ 42nd Inf./Bde. Machine Gun Company

Place	Date	Hour	Summary of Events and Information	Remarks and references to Appendices
ARRAS	1/4/18		Sergeans relieved without incident night of March 31st/April 1st. Further guns effected to strengthen the defences of 42nd Inf/Bde. Our guns put into position in ACHICOURT defences and level crossing on ARRAS-ACHICOURT ROAD.	
ARRAS	2/4/18		Reconnaissance made by Staff Officer 14th Divn. and Officers commanding H.Q. and 42nd Inf/Bde. M.G. Coys to arrange co-operation between Brigades. This is rendered difficult owing to presence of a Regt. of the Gunchiro of the two brigade fronts so that an exchange becomes necessary. Are the existing positions being capable of covering the junction satisfactorily.	
ARRAS	3/4/18		Co-operation arranged with 43rd Inf/Bde M.G Coy in conjunction with Staff Officer 14 Divn. Guns to be raised where guns (Vickers) in front line to cover junction of brigades. Best possible infantry in 42 & 43 Inf/Bde area (D/2s). Arrangements will be made as early as possible to place one of 42 Q Bde guns in this position or else land over position to 43rd Inf/Bdr. Two Hotchkiss rifles and in new erected emplacement in CHATEAU at RONVILLE. Position definitely selo or ridge for covering junction of H1st and H2 8 H2 Inf/Bde.	
ARRAS	4/4/18		OC 168th Bde Inf/Coy taken over the line.	

Army Form C. 2118.

WAR DIARY or INTELLIGENCE SUMMARY

(Erase heading not required.)

Place	Date	Hour	Summary of Events and Information	Remarks and references to Appendices
ARRAS	5/4/16		One man wounded by rifle grenade. Temporary platforms built in parapet sides for Lewis gun positions.	
ARRAS	6/4/16		Two guns in front line relieved by two guns from lines in rear of front line. Relief carried out without incident.	
ARRAS	7/4/16		One officer and three other ranks rejoined from leave to United Kingdom.	
ARRAS	8/4/16		Employment reorganised. One more gun put into RONVILLE DEFENCES. Emplacement started.	
ARRAS	9/4/16		Nothing to report.	
ARRAS	10/4/16		New site chosen to R.E. for a gun in a disused trench to cover ford and approach lines.	
ARRAS	11/4/16		ACHICOURT DEFENCES reconnoitred with a view to defence by machine guns. Eight sites chosen.	
ARRAS	12/4/16		One officer and 2 other ranks proceeded on leave to United Kingdom. Work done on position N.E. of Ronville Cross Roads.	
ARRAS	13/4/16		4 guns relieved without incident on night April 12/13th. Work done in conjunction with R.E. on two emplacements. Also of an emplacement started on one of the eight sites chosen for ACHICOURT DEFENCE scheme.	

Army Form C. 2118.

WAR DIARY
or
INTELLIGENCE SUMMARY
(Erase heading not required.)

Instructions regarding War Diaries and Intelligence Summaries are contained in F. S. Regs., Part II. and the Staff Manual respectively. Title Pages will be prepared in manuscript.

Place	Date	Hour	Summary of Events and Information	Remarks and references to Appendices
ARRAS	14/4/16		2 Platoons completed in ACHICOURT DEFENCES. 2 guns put into these positions. Work done with RE on two emplacements.	
ARRAS	15/4/16		Nothing to report.	
ARRAS	16/4/16		Nothing to report.	
ARRAS	17/4/16		New site for gun on Railway (vis-à-point?:2) chosen to OC 22nd Bn by RE. Plans for new emplacement decided upon at night. New site selected by gun in C.T.A.	
ARRAS	18/4/16		Nothing to report.	
ARRAS	19/4/16		New site selected for a gun in COLINE. Indirect fire brought to bear on NEUVILLE-VITASSE - BEAURAINS ROAD from 9.45pm to 12 midnight, information having been received from a prisoner that a relief used to take place along this road.	
ARRAS	20/4/16		ARRAS shelled during afternoon. House in which Company was billeted hit. Corporal cousin hit, Bgr Lyon killed, two men seriously wounded, three slightly wounded.	
ARRAS	21/4/16		Billets changed to a less shelled area.	

War Diary

May 1916

42nd Brigade Machine Gun Coy.

C. Plowden, Captain
Commanding 42nd Bde Machine Gun Coy

Army Form C. 2118.

WAR DIARY
or
INTELLIGENCE SUMMARY 49th Inf/Bde Lectures for Company

(Erase heading not required.)

Instructions regarding War Diaries and Intelligence Summaries are contained in F.S. Regs., Part II. and the Staff Manual respectively. Title Pages will be prepared in manuscript.

Place	Date	Hour	Summary of Events and Information	Remarks and references to Appendices
ARRAS	1/5/16		Trenches between H29 and H32 temporarily evacuated during bombardment of Nancegs line; two guns placed in company trenches to cover evacuated trenches. Gas guard relieved by night without incident.	
ARRAS	2/5/16		Bigwood has orders to "stand to" from 2am on account of gas alarm, etc. Guns conformed to this order.	
ARRAS	3/5/16		Gun arranged to bear limited covering H.R. line in RONVILLE CHATEAU, etc. Brought to bear on enemy's sap at M5a5t9 by night after bombardment & wire cutting by artillery. Three guns relieved without incident.	*Shul 5.13 MH 3 ARRAS.
ARRAS	4/5/16		Nothing to report.	
ARRAS	5/5/16		Nothing to report.	
ARRAS.	6/5/16		An intended raid on enemy sap at G35.c.8.7 was held up owing to wire being thicker than was at first supposed and consequently L.G. and Lewis supposedly call up artillery. Previous to raid the guns kept up intermittent fire on two saps and another at M6a51.9 to prevent enemy from reinforcing the wire.	*Shul 5.13 MH 3 ARRAS.
ARRAS	7/5/16		Two other bombardiers as reinforcement. Two new positions sited.	

2449 Wt. W14957/M90 750,000 1/16 J.B.C. & A. Forms/C.2118/12.

Army Form C. 2118.

WAR DIARY
or
INTELLIGENCE SUMMARY 22nd Bn/Bn. Lancashire fus Infantry
(Erase heading not required.)

Instructions regarding War Diaries and Intelligence Summaries are contained in F. S. Regs., Part II. and the Staff Manual respectively. Title Pages will be prepared in manuscript.

Place	Date	Hour	Summary of Events and Information	Remarks and references to Appendices
ARRAS	8/5/16		Our own position shelled in ACHICOURT DEFENCES. Two guns fired silenced by sight to check work on trenches destroyed by artillery during afternoon.	
ARRAS	9/5/16		Nothing to report.	
ARRAS	10/5/16		Our own sites for machine guns selected in RONVILLE DEFENCES. Nothing to report.	
ARRAS	11/5/16			
ARRAS	12/5/16		Zeppelins sited in new position under construction in ACHICOURT.	
ARRAS	13/5/16		Special "stand to" ordered 2. 2am – 4.30 am.	
ARRAS	14/5/16		Nothing to report.	
ARRAS	15/5/16		Relief of three guns carried out without incident.	
ARRAS	16/5/16		Nothing to report.	
ARRAS	17/5/16		Fire kept up by sight from first line on German trenches bombarded by artillery during the afternoon.	
ARRAS	18/5/16		Relief of three guns carried out without incident.	

Army Form C. 2118.

WAR DIARY
or
INTELLIGENCE SUMMARY 42nd Inf. Bde. Machine Gun Coy.

(Erase heading not required.)

Instructions regarding War Diaries and Intelligence Summaries are contained in F. S. Regs., Part II. and the Staff Manual respectively. Title Pages will be prepared in manuscript.

Place	Date	Hour	Summary of Events and Information	Remarks and references to Appendices
ARRAS	19/5/16		Two guns changed positions from front line being changing with front line N/guns.	
ARRAS	20/5/16		Nothing to report.	
ARRAS	21/5/16		Two guns relieved without incident.	
ARRAS	22/5/16		Nothing to report.	
ARRAS	23/5/16		One other rank sent to hospital acting steline suffering from burn in the eyes and face received while at duty. Three guns relieved without incident.	
ARRAS	24/5/16		Changes of positions of guns in the front and other lines effected without incident. Nothing to report.	
ARRAS	25/5/16		Preliminary reconnaissance of employing positions from which to shoot at certain selected points in the enemy's lines. Three guns relieved without incident.	
ARRAS	27/5/16		Platforms erected for future use at points selected on 25th.	
ARRAS	28/5/16		Arrangements for night firing completed. 1800 rounds fired at Sep 2 having been signed to prevent enemy repairing damage done by artillery.	x Sheet 51.73 G 35-267
ARRAS	29/5/16		Three guns relieved without incident.	

2449 Wt. W14957/M90 750,000 1/16 J.B.C. & A. Forms/C.2118/12.

Army Form C. 2118.

WAR DIARY
or
INTELLIGENCE SUMMARY

42nd Inf/Bde Machine Gun Coy.

(Erase heading not required.)

Instructions regarding War Diaries and Intelligence Summaries are contained in F. S. Regs., Part II. and the Staff Manual respectively. Title Pages will be prepared in manuscript.

Place	Date	Hour	Summary of Events and Information	Remarks and references to Appendices
ARRAS	28/6/16	1am – 1.30am	Heavy shelling of front line for 20 minutes & Lys battalion fired from F.O.P. 1/5/1 Prailes (BEAURAINS – ACHICOURT ROAD) withdrawn to support during bombardment and resumed immediately shelling had stopped. Gun kept up chy fire on the wire in front of damaged trenches to check any attempt at a raid or the part of the enemy. Captured and one private of War gun team slightly wounded.	

G.F. Plunder Capt.
Comdg 42 D Inf/Bde M.G. Coy.

Army Form C.2118.

WAR DIARY
or
INTELLIGENCE SUMMARY

48th (6h)/Bn Machine Gun Coy. Vol 4

XIV

(Erase heading not required.)

Instructions regarding War Diaries and Intelligence Summaries are contained in F.S. Regs., Part II. and the Staff Manual respectively. Title Pages will be prepared in manuscript.

Place	Date	Hour	Summary of Events and Information	Remarks and references to Appendices
ARRAS	1/6/16		Reconnaissance of new positions and alternative positions for existing emplacements.	
ARRAS	2/6/16		Teaghers changed positions without incident. Three guns relieved without incident. On man slightly wounded on 31/5/16 returned from ambulance.	
ARRAS	3/6/16		Lieutenant asked for new Lewis gun position at SCHICOURT – BEAURAINS ROAD also new emplacement.	
ARRAS	4/6/16		Nothing to report.	
ARRAS	5/6/16		Tangens changed positions without incident.	
ARRAS	6/6/16		Nothing to report. Three guns relieved without incident.	
ARRAS	7/6/16		Nothing to report.	
ARRAS	8/6/16		Two guns changed positions without incident.	
ARRAS	9/6/16		Four guns relieved without incident.	
ARRAS	10/6/16		Nothing to report.	
ARRAS	11/6/16		Nothing to report.	
ARRAS	12/6/16		Four guns relieved without incident.	
ARRAS	13/6/16		Tangens changed positions without incident.	
ARRAS	14/6/16		Nothing to report.	

WAR DIARY or INTELLIGENCE SUMMARY

Army Form C. 2118.

42 L'dy/Bde R.J.Cy

Place	Date	Hour	Summary of Events and Information	Remarks and references to Appendices
ARRAS	15/6/16		Nothing to report.	
ARRAS	16/6/16.		Two dugouts finally sited in gun emplacements. Four guns relieved without incident.	
ARRAS	17/6/16.		Four guns changed positions without incident. Reinforcement of 10 other ranks joined Battery including one saddler.	
ARRAS	18/6/16.		Reconnaissance of front & support battalion of 95th Inf/Bde with OC 3rd Bde R.J.Cy. Two positions decided on for occupation by guns of 42 L'dy Bde R.J.Cy on relief. Two positions occupied by morning found. Other positions to occur after dawn.	
ARRAS	19/6/16.		Two guns relieved without incident.	
ARRAS	20/6/16.		Two guns moved into position on relief of 95 3 L'dy/Bde R.J.Cy in accordance with 42 L.Bde OOs. Positions situated in JB Line and ST SAUVEUR DEFENCES.	
ARRAS	21/6/16.		Two guns changed position in the line without incident.	
ARRAS	22/6/16.		Two guns relieved without incident.	
ARRAS	23/6/16.		Two guns changed positions without incident.	
ARRAS	24/6/16.		Wire kept up all night on our left Coy Lt L? Lere and in front of enemy's known by artillery during the afternoon.	
ARRAS	25/6/16.		Firing by guns at 02 24/6/16 at various targets.	
ARRAS	26/6/16		as for 24/6/16 and 25/6/16.	

Army Form C. 2118.

WAR DIARY
or
INTELLIGENCE SUMMARY 42nd Inf. Bde. Machine Gun Company

(Erase heading not required.)

Instructions regarding War Diaries and Intelligence Summaries are contained in F. S. Regs., Part II. and the Staff Manual respectively. Title Pages will be prepared in manuscript.

Place	Date	Hour	Summary of Events and Information	Remarks and references to Appendices
ARRAS	27/6/16	3.8pm – 3.46p	Three guns firing on enemy parapets or places of gun emplacements opposite the village of BEAURAINS at 3pm. The guns firing all night or same point as previous three nights	X See sketch
ARRAS.	28/6/16		Fire kept up all night on same object as on preceding nights and two other places in addition, viz new and by arty from M5c 0-3½ — M5c a-5-8. and M4 a 5-2	X See Sketch Reft– 9MRH3
ARRAS	29/6/16		Very heavy firing in connection with raid by 5th Ox/Bucks LI by Capt Bagnell (see summary for 28/6/16) The other emplacement commenced firing at 9.40 side of BOMVILLE BEAURAINS ROAD. Barrage party report that they found enemy wiring party engaged with wire in one cut and jugs through which forty killed and wounded.	St BMW 3 Retched Rd 1/10000
ARRAS.	2/7/16		Fire kept up for 12 MN throughout hours of darkness or same point as on 24th & 25th and succeeding nights.	

42nd INF. BRIGADE,
MACHINE GUN
COMPANY.
No. ....
Date 2/7/16

G. L. Pleadin Capt.
Cmg 42 Inf Bde M.G. Coy.

CONFIDENTIAL.

WAR DIARY.

42ND MACHINE GUN COMPANY.

1st – 31st JULY 1916.

Army Form C. 2118.

WAR DIARY
or
INTELLIGENCE SUMMARY

42nd Machine Gun Company

(Erase heading not required.)

Instructions regarding War Diaries and Intelligence Summaries are contained in F.S. Regs., Part II. and the Staff Manual respectively. Title Pages will be prepared in manuscript.

Place	Date	Hour	Summary of Events and Information	Remarks and references to Appendices
ARRAS	1/7/16		Fire opened by two guns on German parapets during discharge of smoke cloud.	
ARRAS	2/7/16		Nothing to report.	
ARRAS	3/7/16		Fire kept up for two hours by 2 guns on enemy dumps on and near BEAURAINS – TILLOY ROAD. Guns are sited in H.S. Line.	
ARRAS	4/7/16		Two guns relieved without incident.	
ARRAS	5/7/16		Fire opened on same target as on 3/7/16. Two guns changed positions without incident.	
ARRAS	6/7/16		Fire kept up for two hours from 12 M.N. on cross roads.	
ARRAS	7/7/16		Reconnaissance for alternative positions. Two guns relieved without incident.	
ARRAS	8/7/16		Fire opened on enemy dumps by 2 gs (M.11.a.2.6 – M.11.a.6.4.9 and 9 between.) ×	× Trench maps ARRAS 51 B N.W. 3
ARRAS	9/7/16		Fire opened on TELEGRAPH HILL (77 mm battery) 10.30pm – 12 midnight.	Sheets 2 B 1/10000
ARRAS	10/7/16		Two guns relieved without incident. Fire opened on enemy dumps by 2 gs (M.5.b.9.5 – M.6.c.2.7.) ×	
ARRAS	11/7/16		Fire kept up during hours of darkness to enfilade enemy trenches, withdrawal being effected by artillery and 9 trench mortars (M.11.c.3.7 – 6.6. and M.4 d 5.6 – 3.4.) ×	

WAR DIARY or INTELLIGENCE SUMMARY

Army Form C. 2118.

112th Machine Gun Company

Place	Date	Hour	Summary of Events and Information	Remarks and references to Appendices
ARRAS	12/7/16		One gun protected sector (destroyed) by shell fire; two other racks mounted. Two teams changed positions without incident. Fire as per M.G.B. by night. Alterations to the loopholes carried out to give new line of fire.	
ARRAS	13/7/16		Machine gunning enemy night to the flank of area to be raided.	
ARRAS	14/7/16		Two guns firing at enemy parapets during S.A.A. cloud 2.50am – 3.30am. Two teams changed positions without incident. One gun cookhouse gas line (V68) turned on to TELEGRAPH HILL by enemy barrage.	
ARRAS	15/7/16		One officer & two other ranks attached for instruction from 33rd Bgd. Fire opened on TELEGRAPH HILL	
ARRAS	16/7/16 17/7/16		One gun stood by in temporary position ready to barrage enemy front line between T. Sann & I. Green 17, in case of success of raiding party to enter hostile trenches before 7am. Fire not required or raid abandoned owing to wire not being cut.	
	17/7/16		Fire by M.G. on TELEGRAPH HILL 77mm battery 9.45pm – 11pm	

WAR DIARY
or
INTELLIGENCE SUMMARY

Army Form C. 2118.

42nd Declines for Coy

Place	Date	Hour	Summary of Events and Information	Remarks and references to Appendices
ARRAS	18/7/16		Two teams changed positions without incident. Fire opened on following targets by night. Telephone exchange in US Sns at M5.9.52. Crumps at M6c 3.8. and 9 M5b.9.6 Trench tramway junction at M6c.6.9½.	
ARRAS	19/7/16		Fire opened on road from TILLOY at H.31.c, junction of communication trenches at G.36.a.9.5.1, and TELEGRAPH HILL by night.	
ARRAS	20/7/16		Two guns relieved without incident. Fire opened by night on BEAURAINS - TILLOY Road.	
ARRAS	21/7/16		Company Runner killed in rear area for 33rd Inf Bde M.G. Coy. Reconnaissance of I Left Sector M.G. positions.	
ARRAS	22/7/16		Six guns in A sector relieved by Coy by 33rd Inf Bde M.G. Coy. Officer by night by Coy in I Left Sector by day.	
ARRAS	23/7/16		Nothing to report.	
ARRAS	24/7/16		Our new position occupied in ST SAUVEUR. Fire opened by night on C.16.b.9 - H.13.a.3.3 - H.13.D.8.4. Artillery to support.	

Army Form C. 2118.

WAR DIARY
or
INTELLIGENCE SUMMARY   42nd Machine Gun Company

(Erase heading not required.)

Instructions regarding War Diaries and Intelligence Summaries are contained in F. S. Regs., Part II. and the Staff Manual respectively. Title Pages will be prepared in manuscript.

Place	Date	Hour	Summary of Events and Information	Remarks and references to Appendices
ARRAS	26/7/16		Reth. Relieving arrangements made for relief of all guns in sector by VI Corps. 2 g By and 33" Bde 2g Coy. 54 Bn wheels from Battalions of 42 & Bde.	
ARRAS	27/7/16		All guns relieved by mgts 2 g By and 33" Bde 2g Coy. Coy marched from ARRAS to DUISANS and bivouacked there for night.	
DUISANS 28/7/16 & Gde ROLLECOURT	28/7/16		Company marched from DUISANS to GRANDE ROLLECOURT and billetted there for night. Eighteen men fell out, all guns gained except three distance about 9 miles. Weather very intense.	
Gde ROLLECOURT – MEZEROLLES	29/7/16		Company marched from GRANDE ROLLECOURT to MEZEROLLES. Sixty seven men fell out, all rejoined in evening except three. distance about 12 miles. Weather very intense.	
MEZEROLLES	30/7/16		Training of attached men continued. Cable training of old hands continued. Rifle parade. All men who fell out previous day rejoined except one.	
MEZEROLLES – FIENVILLERS	31/7/16		Marched out from MEZEROLLES 7.15 am, reached FIENVILLERS 10 am. 5½ miles. One man fell out who rejoined immediately.	

W.F. Plunder Capt.
Comdg 42 MG Machine Gun Coy.

42nd Brigade.
14th Division.

42nd BRIGADE.

MACHINE GUN COMPANY

AUGUST 1 9 1 6

vol 6

WAR DIARY

42ⁿᵈ MACHINE GUN COY

VOL VI

August 1916.

WAR DIARY
or
INTELLIGENCE SUMMARY   49 Machine Gun Company

Army Form C. 2118.

Vol. 6.

(Erase heading not required.)

Place	Date	Hour	Summary of Events and Information	Remarks and references to Appendices
FIENVILLERS	1/8/16		Training continued.	
FIENVILLERS	2/8/16		Training continued.	
FIENVILLERS	3/8/16		Training continued.	
FIENVILLERS	4/8/16		Training continued.	
FIENVILLERS	5/8/16		Training continued.	
FIENVILLERS	6/8/16		1st Line Transport moved from FIENVILLERS — CARDONETTE.	
FIENVILLERS	7/8/16		Remainder by train from FIENVILLERS — BUIRE-sur-L'ANCRE.	
BUIRE-sur-L'ANCRE	8/8/16		Training continued.	
BUIRE sur L'ANCRE	9/8/16		Training continued.	
BUIRE sur L'ANCRE	10/8/16		Training continued.	
BUIRE sur L'ANCRE	11/8/16		Training continued.	
DIVISIONAL RESERVE near FRICOURT	12/8/16		Moved from BUIRE sur L'ANCRE to bivouacs near FRICOURT and became Divisional Reserve.	

WAR DIARY or INTELLIGENCE SUMMARY

Army Form C. 2118.

149 Company Machine Gun Corps

(Erase heading not required.)

Place	Date	Hour	Summary of Events and Information	Remarks and references to Appendices
Near FRICOURT	13/8/16		Training continued	
"	14/8/16		Training continued	
"	15/8/16		Reconnaissance of DELVILLE WOOD machine gun positions. Training continued	
"	16/8/16		" " " "	
"	17/8/16		Reconnaissance of route to DELVILLE WOOD via CRUCIFIX ALLEY, LONGTRENCH - PILL TRENCH. Training continued	
"	18/8/16		Company marching by platoons at 2.45 p.m. to arrive at half an hours notice while attack by 143rd Bde & 141st Inf Bdes and advanced decisions were in progress. Company moved to MONTAUBAN. Guides formed MONTAUBAN DEFENCES. Four guns relieved six of 143rd by starting at 10.30pm. Positions as follows — 4 in front line in new trenches taken previous day by 143 Bde: 2 in DELVILLE WOOD: 1 in reserve at Battn HQ Sec	3184·92·5 −7.785·4½ −3150
MONTAUBAN and trenches in rear and DELVILLE WOOD	19/8/16			
" "	20/8/16		Whole line including HQ subjected shelled during day. One OR wounded, two slightly shell shock. One gun destroyed by shellfire.	

WAR DIARY or INTELLIGENCE SUMMARY

Army Form C. 2118.

HQ 8 Machine Gun Company

(Erase heading not required.)

Place	Date	Hour	Summary of Events and Information	Remarks and references to Appendices
MONTAUBAN and trenches near DELVILLE WOOD	21/8/16		2nd Lts Reece & Shields & Bryant find in conjunction with kiwis visit OR dgout and 1 Left. Two Orderlies wounded while carrying messages. Two OR killed & two wounded during night.	
" "	22/8/16		2nd Lts A. T. W. [?] & [?] Boyd & Lts changed places to conform with change of places of 2nd Lts ? & ? Bleus the previous night. One Officer still shock cases, two OR wounded.	
" "	23/8/16		Arrangements made for co-operation with machine operation. Site selected for indirect fire on SWITCH TRENCH from S4 b 0.3 to S5 & 10.92. Four OR wounded.	Ref 8/100/9 French 2nd Govt
" "	24/8/16		Attack by 48 & 1/1 Bde on German trenches in and beyond DELVILLE WOOD was postponed as follows: 4 guns hitherto employed firing from (Devils Trench) 2 guns each allotted to three approaching batteries 2 guns in reserve of Right & Left Bn of the W.R. FS. 1 gun in Bde Reserve 3 guns firing indirect on target arranged for 23/8/16.	

Army Form C. 2118.

WAR DIARY
or
INTELLIGENCE SUMMARY 42d Lancashire Infantry
(Erase heading not required.)

Instructions regarding War Diaries and Intelligence Summaries are contained in F.S. Regs., Part II. and the Staff Manual respectively. Title Pages will be prepared in manuscript.

Place	Date	Hour	Summary of Events and Information	Remarks and references to Appendices
Trenches DELVILLE WOOD	24/8/16	5:45 p.m.	Our guns firing inferred opened fire. Guns behaved to battalions extending lines over behind this were with the exception of the two specialist Lewis gun battle which were about to join the reserve company to our original front line, one of those subsequently non placed. The other remained behind in support. The original above were for the final seven projected which in support. It formed in the first seven lines the other to be projected to the trenches where hours of as far as ready for occupation. These worked subsequently to be modified, owing to final objectives not being gained also along the road. The final position of support in seven projected to be German front lines, now in practice is somewhat less as our our original front line. The firm in reserve a top Battalion The F.W. was burned up the following Railway to cover the rear of the left flank at the FLERS ROAD. Inferred fire was kept up intermittently all night by the two guns before detailed. Total casualties during the engagement 1 officer slightly wounded. 1 OR wounded 10 killed 6 OR Killed, 11 OR wounded. H OR Missing.	

Army Form C. 2118.

WAR DIARY
or
INTELLIGENCE SUMMARY
(Erase heading not required.)

HQ 2 Rachen Jn Coy [?]

Place	Date	Hour	Summary of Events and Information	Remarks and references to Appendices
DELVILLE WOOD	25/9/16		Slight alterations made in the placing of one gun in new post. No enemy reaction but attention is locked attention.	
DELVILLE WOOD and Bivouacs near FRICOURT.	26/9/16		Company relieved by 43rd Coy in DELVILLE WOOD trenches. Reached back to bivouacs near FRICOURT.	
Near FRICOURT	27/9/16		Coy rested. Guns cleaned and overhauled.	
Rear FRICOURT	28/9/16		Nothing to report.	
Rear FRICOURT	29/9/16		Nothing to report. Training ordered.	
DERNAN-COURT	30/9/16		Coy marched from bivouacs near FRICOURT to DERNANCOURT.	

Army Form C. 2118.

WAR DIARY
or
INTELLIGENCE SUMMARY 42ⁿᵈ Machine Gun Company.

(Erase heading not required.)

Place	Date	Hour	Summary of Events and Information	Remarks and references to Appendices
DERNANCOURT -AVESNES	31/8/16		Company less transport entrained at DERNANCOURT and detrained at AIRAINES, transport marched from AIRAINES to billets at AVESNES. Transport followed by road.	

A.J. Pheasher Capt.
Comdg 42ⁿᵈ M.G. Coy.

Vol 7

WAR DIARY

42nd Machine Gun Company

for SEPTEMBER 1916

Volume VII

Army Form C. 2118.

WAR DIARY
or
INTELLIGENCE SUMMARY 42nd Machine Gun Company
(Erase heading not required.)

Place	Date	Hour	Summary of Events and Information	Remarks and references to Appendices
ARMY G.Lodr.	27/9/16		Work started on new mine dugout.	
"	28/9/16		Work continued on mine dugout. Some slight alterations made in gun positions.	
"	29/9/16		Work continued on mine dugout and 2 new guns started.	
G.Lodr.	30/9/16		Work continued on mine dugout and two new mine dugouts.	

L.H. Pheralen Capt.
Cmdg 42nd M.G. Coy.

1/10/16.

Army Form C. 2118.

WAR DIARY
or
INTELLIGENCE SUMMARY

42ⁿᵈ Machine Gun Company

(Erase heading not required.)

Instructions regarding War Diaries and Intelligence Summaries are contained in F. S. Regs., Part II. and the Staff Manual respectively. Title Pages will be prepared in manuscript.

Place	Date	Hour	Summary of Events and Information	Remarks and references to Appendices
DERNANCOURT	19/9/16		Training continued. 2 S.O.R. joined the Company.	
"	20/9/16		Training continued.	
"	21/9/16		Transport marched from DERNANCOURT en route for GRAND RULLECOURT.	
DERNANCOURT – GRAND RULLECOURT	22/9/16		Company moved by bus to GRAND RULLECOURT.	
GRAND RULLECOURT	23/9/16		Training continued.	
GRAND RULLECOURT – BERNEVILLE	24/9/16		Company marched to BERNEVILLE. Reconnaissance of G Sector (AGNY).	
G Sector (AGNY)	25/9/16		Company took over 2 Gun positions from 86ᵗʰ M.G. Coy by night.	
"	26/9/16		Nothing to report.	

Army Form C. 2118.

WAR DIARY
or
INTELLIGENCE SUMMARY

22nd Machine Gun Company

(Erase heading not required.)

Instructions regarding War Diaries and Intelligence Summaries are contained in F. S. Regs., Part II. and the Staff Manual respectively. Title Pages will be prepared in manuscript.

Place	Date	Hour	Summary of Events and Information	Remarks and references to Appendices
FRICOURT	13/9/16		Nothing to report.	
FRICOURT - MONTAUBAN	14/9/16		Company marched in the evening to the forward area and split up into its separate teams in accordance with operation orders for following attack.	
	15/9/16		Company took part in attack on former lines. 8 guns detailed, two to each battalion. 8 guns followed in rear of two rear battalions for use after final objective had been reached. Final objective was not reached. Several guns came into action during the day at various targets. Four mobile field guns were put out of action by machine gun fire. Heavy counter attack at 9 p.m. repulsed. Secret put up by machine gun fire. Casualties 2 officers & other ranks. Guns relieved during the night by 43 M.G. Coy.	
Near FRICOURT	17/9/16		Company rested at MONTAUBAN till night and marched to camp near FRICOURT.	
Near DERNANCOURT	18/9/16		Company marched to camp near DERNANCOURT.	

10 OR (joined Company).

Army Form C. 2118.

WAR DIARY
or
INTELLIGENCE SUMMARY

42ⁿᵈ Lackum from Cropsey

(Erase heading not required.)

Place	Date	Hour	Summary of Events and Information	Remarks and references to Appendices
AVESNES	1/9/16		Training continued.	
"	2/9/16		Having arrived draft of 10 O.R. joined	
"	3/9/16		draft of 14 O.R. joined.	
"	4/9/16		Training continued.	
"	5/9/16		Training continued.	
"	6/9/16		Having continued.	
"	7/9/16		Training continued.	
"	8/9/16		Training continued.	
"	9/9/16		Training continued.	
"	10/9/16		Transport shed by road to billets at ALLEY sur SOMME en route to DERNANCOURT.	
AVESNES –DERNANCOURT	11/9/16		Company entrained at AVESNES and detrained at MERICOURT & marched to camp near DERNANCOURT	
near FRICOURT	12/9/16		Company marched from DERNANCOURT to camp near FRICOURT.	

Vol 8

War Diary.

42nd Machine Gun Company.

Vol VIII.   Oct. 1916.

Army Form C. 2118.

WAR DIARY
or
INTELLIGENCE SUMMARY 42nd Machine Gun Company

(Erase heading not required.)

Instructions regarding War Diaries and Intelligence Summaries are contained in F. S. Regs., Part II. and the Staff Manual respectively. Title Pages will be prepared in manuscript.

Place	Date	Hour	Summary of Events and Information	Remarks and references to Appendices
G. Seda AGNY	1/10/16		Work continued on dugouts.	
"	2/10/16		Relief carried out by Coy. without incident. Work continued on dugouts.	
"	3/10/16		Work continued on dugouts.	
"	4/10/16		Work continued on dugouts and one new lookout started.	
"	5/10/16		Work continued on all new dugouts.	
"	6/10/16		Work continued on new dugouts.	
"	7/10/16		Work continued on new dugouts.	
"	8/10/16		Work continued on new dugouts and one new dugout started	
"	9/10/16		Relief carried out by day without incident. Work continued on dugouts.	
"	10/10/16		Dugouts continued	
"	11/10/16		Dugouts continued and 4 of 6 platforms built.	
"	12/10/16		Dugouts continued and Gas Screens put up at 2 old dugouts	
"	13/10/16		Work on dugouts and Gas Screens continued.	
"	14/10/16		Dugouts continued.	
"	15/10/16		Dugouts and Gas Screens continued	
"	16/10/16		Dugouts and Gas Screens Continued	
"	17/10/16			

Army Form C. 2118.

WAR DIARY
~~INTELLIGENCE SUMMARY~~
(Erase heading not required.)

of 49th Machine Gun Company

Place	Date	Hour	Summary of Events and Information	Remarks and references to Appendices
R. SECTOR AGNY	18/10/16		Work on Dugouts and Gas screens continued. 6000 rounds were fired by 2 guns of 17%/18th throughout the night at gaps in the enemy's wire.	
"	19/10/16		Work on Dugouts and Gas screens continued. 5000 rounds were fired by 2 guns throughout the night of 18th/19th at gaps in the enemy's wire.	
"	20/10/16		Dugouts and Gas screens continued. 4800 rounds fired by 2 guns at enemy's wire throughout night 19th/20th.	
"	21/10/16		Work continued on Dugouts and Gas Screens.	
"	22/10/16		Work continued on Dugouts and Gas Screens.	
"	23/10/16		Work continued on Dugouts and Gas Screens.	
"	24/10/16			
"	25/10/16		Relief carried out without incident.	
"	26/10/16		Ol 36th Coy came to arrange details of relief.	
"	27/10/16		Coy relieved by 36th Coy by 6 a.m. Relief carried out without incident.	
WARQUETIN	27/10/16		Coy marched from WARQUETIN to LIENCOURT.	
LIENCOURT	28/10/16		Inspection of R.E. clothing gun &c. Attached Buen Roll through depth of proper	
"	29/10/16		R. with Church Parade.	
"	30/10/16		Training continued.	
"	31/10/16		Training continued.	

G.P. Meeder Capt.
Commanding 49nd Machine Gun Coy.

Confidential

Vol 9

War Diary

of

42nd Machine Gun Company.

***   ***   ***   ***   ***

From 1st Nov 1916 to 30th Nov 1916.

(Volume 9)

Army Form C. 2118.

WAR DIARY
or
INTELLIGENCE SUMMARY 42nd Machine Gun Company
(Erase heading not required.)

Instructions regarding War Diaries and Intelligence Summaries are contained in F. S. Regs., Part II. and the Staff Manual respectively. Title Pages will be prepared in manuscript.

Place	Date	Hour	Summary of Events and Information	Remarks and references to Appendices
LIENCOURT	1/11/16		Training continued.	
"	2/11/16		Training continued.	
"	3/11/16		Training continued. Forty other ranks joined for attachment & training.	
"	4/11/16		Training continued.	
"	5/11/16		Church parade.	
"	6/11/16		Training continued. Thirty nine other Ranks returned to Base Depot under the established scheme.	
"	7/11/16		Training continued.	
"	8/11/16		Training continued.	
"	9/11/16		Training continued.	
"	10/11/16		Training continued.	
"	11/11/16		Training continued.	
"	12/11/16		Church Parade.	
"	13/11/16		Training continued.	
"	14/11/16		Training continued.	
"	15/11/16		Training continued.	

Army Form C. 2118.

WAR DIARY
or
INTELLIGENCE SUMMARY

192 Machine Gun Company

(Erase heading not required.)

Instructions regarding War Diaries and Intelligence Summaries are contained in F. S. Regs., Part II. and the Staff Manual respectively. Title Pages will be prepared in manuscript.

Place	Date	Hour	Summary of Events and Information	Remarks and references to Appendices
LIENCOURT	14/11/16		Training continued.	
"	15/11/16		Training continued.	
"	16/11/16		Training continued. Church Parade	
"	19/11/16		Training continued.	
"	20/11/16		Training continued.	
"	21/11/16		Training continued.	
"	22/11/16		Training continued.	
LIENCOURT –GOUY EN ARTOIS	23/11/16		Company marched from LIENCOURT to GOUY EN ARTOIS	
GOUY EN ARTOIS	24/11/16		Training continued.	
"	25/11/16		Training continued. Church Parade.	
"	26/11/16		Training continued. 30 Officers & OR innoculated.	
"	27/11/16		Training continued.	
"	28/11/16		Training continued.	
"	29/11/16		Training continued. All ranks fitted with new respirators.	[signature] Lt OC 192 MGC

WAR DIARY.

CONFIDENTIAL.

UNIT. 42nd Machine Gun Company.

PERIOD. From Dec. 1st 1916 To Dec 31st 1916

VOLUME NO. 10

Vol 10

Army Form C. 2118.

WAR DIARY
or
INTELLIGENCE SUMMARY.

(Erase heading not required.)

142nd Machine Gun Company

Instructions regarding War Diaries and Intelligence Summaries are contained in F.S. Regs., Part II. and the Staff Manual respectively. Title pages will be prepared in manuscript.

Place	Date	Hour	Summary of Events and Information	Remarks and references to Appendices
COUP en ARTOIS	1/12/16		Training continued.	
"	2/12/16		Training continued. Church Parade.	
"	3/12/16		Training continued. Range taking test.	
"	4/12/16		Inspection by B.G.C. 42nd Inf. Bde.	
"	5/12/16		Training continued.	
"	6/12/16		Training continued.	
"	7/12/16		Company marched from COUP EN ARTOIS to LIGNEREUIL	
COUP en ARTOIS — LIGNEREUIL	8/12/16			
LIGNEREUIL	9/12/16		Training continued. Church Parade.	
"	10/12/16			
"	11/12/16		Training continued.	
"	12/12/16		Training continued. Preliminary arrangements made for relief of 95th Coy in G Sector.	
"	13/12/16		Inspection of small box respirators and I have respirator drill by Divisional Gas Officer.	
"	14/12/16		Training continued.	
"	15/12/16		Company marched to DAINVILLE.	

Army Form C. 2118.

WAR DIARY
or
INTELLIGENCE SUMMARY.   H.Q. 2nd Wing R.F.C.

(Erase heading not required.)

Instructions regarding War Diaries and Intelligence Summaries are contained in F.S. Regs., Part II. and the Staff Manual respectively. Title pages will be prepared in manuscript.

Place	Date	Hour	Summary of Events and Information	Remarks and references to Appendices
AGNY (G. Sector) II Corps Front	16/12/16		Company relieved 36th Coy in G Sector by day. Guns in Support Line, Reserve Line, Keep guns in AGNY DEFENCES, front guns set up to places to other emplacements in AGNY DEFENCES.	
"	17/12/16		Guns harassed fire & ranged on various targets which Germans had during afternoon. 1000 rounds fired at selected targets which Germans had lately be occupying.	
"	17/12/16		2/m harassing fire on back areas fired 2 R by van guns and at 9 a/pm. Germans shelled enemy's back areas fired 2 R by van guns and at 9 a/pm. Germans shelled	
"	18/12/16		Three guns fired by a/pl on selected targets in enemy's back area. 1000 rounds fired.	
"	19/12/16		Reconnaissance of enemy positions 2 May very satisfactory found. Work by guns.	
"	20/12/16		2 May to repeat. Except Work 2 guns.	
"	21/12/16		Work 2 guns in Batteries.	
"	22/12/16		Further reconnaissance of enemy positions. English found 9 A. Work to cover found between Battery & G.12. Relief by gun teams. Our positions for which fire secured.	
"	23/12/16		Work achieved Work by guns.	
"	24/12/16			
"	25/12/16		Work on Dugouts continued. Reconnaissance started from A beyond to our emplacement. Work 12 guns continued. Positions selected for which to harass enemy's rear.	
"	26/12/16		...lines in rear of German trenches.	
"	27/12/16		Work achieved 12 Dugouts. 1000 Rds fired by a/pl Pl 21 C.40. - 2.27 & 42.	× 2 of MÉRICOURT L'ABBÉ Ph... R.F.P. Hoaxes
"	28/12/16		Work advanced on Dugouts in preparation, Dugouts continued. 1000 rounds fired by a/pl at Rd & M 21 C. 1000 & Rd & 9 & Rd & 9 & M 27 a.	

WAR DIARY
or
INTELLIGENCE SUMMARY.

Army Form C. 2118.

49². Machine Gun Coy.

Place	Date	Hour	Summary of Events and Information	Remarks and references to Appendices
H.Q. Scala r/Capo Fort	2/9/16		Both R. dugouts enfiladed. Firing by night or enemy's back areas.	
-	8/9/16		Five dugouts reoccupied & Barrage by McAbre. Both enfiladed on targets. Firing by night or back areas.	
-	9/9/16		One Gun damaged & temporary emplacement entirely collapsed. Repairs to damaged dugouts carried out. Fire kept up for a long range barrage to assist Somersets and by bijah on the left. Up Gr. 12 R.r. enfilt hostile machine gun fire on enemy's back area.	

L. Thomson Major
Oy 49² MyC

WAR DIARY.

CONFIDENTIAL.

UNIT,   42nd Machine Gun Company.

PERIOD. From 1st Jan 1917   To 31st Jan 1917

VOLUME NO.

Army Form C. 2118.

WAR DIARY
or
INTELLIGENCE SUMMARY
(Erase heading not required.)

42nd M.G. Coy

Place	Date	Hour	Summary of Events and Information	Remarks and references to Appendices
Epéhy Sector in opns.	1/1/17		Guns laid for indirect day range barrage to co-operate with intended raid and by Brigade on the left. Raid postponed.	
"	2/1/17		Both artilleries on our beyond to and repair to something road. Fire opened by S.A.A. on selected spots in enemy's back areas by night, also on light dumps by day.	
"	3/1/17		Work continued as before.	
"	4/1/17		Work carried on beyond to 2000 rounds fired a selected targets by day and by night.	
"	5/1/17		Work continued as beyond.	
"	6/1/17 3.8p -4.2p		Barrage with spare on area which S.H. + his had resulted by 43rd Inf. Bde. on the left of Ecoust (21,500 Rds). Fire kept up during the night by these guns on the same area 7500 rounds fired.	
"	7/1/17		Relief of our teams carried out without incident. 1000 rounds fired by night on same areas as on 6 cur. V.	

WAR DIARY

Army Form C. 2118.

Intelligence Summary

42nd M.G. Coy

Place	Date	Hour	Summary of Events and Information	Remarks and references to Appendices
C. Secte 41 left sub sec.	7/1/17		Both ordered on new targets. 10000 rounds fired between 6pm & Midnight 8/1/17 on same targets as two previous nights.	
"	8/1/17		Both continued on same targets.	
"	9/1/17		Both continued on same targets. 2000 rounds fired at areas behind the enemy's lines 5pm - 7pm.	
"	10/1/17		Both continued on same targets.	
"	11/1/17		Both continued on same targets. 2000 rounds fired on area behind by the enemy during the afternoon. (Trench tramway between M15.b.60.55. & M15.d.50.20.)* Artillery during the afternoon fired by aph in enemy trenches M26.c.5.5.x. Both continued on same targets. 2000 rounds fired.	*Trench by Tramway NEUVILLE-VITASSE "
"	12/1/17		Relief of gun teams carried out without incident. Preliminary reconnaissance of p.p.p's in area from which to cooperate in forthcoming operations in front of Points 106 & 2 Rainbows in case of hostile attack.	
"	13/1/17		Both continued on same targets. Fired special bursts of fire at R. M14.c.57 when orders had been repeated enemy shown interest in our targets.	
"	14/1/17			

Army Form C. 2118.

WAR DIARY
or
INTELLIGENCE SUMMARY.

(Erase heading not required.)

42nd M.G. Coy

Place	Date	Hour	Summary of Events and Information	Remarks and references to Appendices
C Sect. 14 Coy 2nd Div.	16/1/17		Work carried on dug outs. 2000 Rounds fired by Day at M23 & S.9. Their movement has apparently been reported by Day.	French Regt 1/Somme
"	17/1/17		Work carried on dug outs. 1000 rounds searching fired at 21.c.5.3 - M27 a.3.2. by night.	MIRVILLE VITASSE
"	18/1/17		Work carried on dug outs. 2000 rounds fired by Day on Rail at M25 B.39. 200 rounds by night at German support line M5 b.56 - M5 c.5.9. 2000 rounds by night at road & dumps M21c 7.5. 4.15pm 220 rounds at hostile aeroplane.	
"	19/1/17		Work carried on dug outs. 2000 rounds fired between 6pm & 10pm at dumps M21 C.H.3 & road near by.	" "
"	20/1/17		Relief of teams carried out without incident.	" "
"	21/1/17		Work carried on Dug outs. 2000 rounds fired between 5 & 9.30 pm on enemy second line from M4.d - M.5 a & b.	
"	22/1/17		Work continued on Dug outs. 1900 rounds fired at hostile aircraft.	

Army Form C. 2118.

WAR DIARY
or
INTELLIGENCE SUMMARY
(Erase heading not required.)

42nd M.G. Coy

Instructions regarding War Diaries and Intelligence Summaries are contained in F.S. Regs., Part II. and the Staff Manual respectively. Title pages will be prepared in manuscript.

Place	Date	Hour	Summary of Events and Information	Remarks and references to Appendices
Ly Sect of VII Corps front	23/1/17		Work on Dugouts stopped through lack of Material. 5pm – 9pm 1250 rounds fired on Sunken road between M.15.d & M.27.a. 1150 rounds fired at Hostile Aircraft.	Ref NEUVILLE VITASSE Trench Map 1 : 10,000.
	24/1/17		No work on Dugouts. 4:30pm – 6:30pm 1000 rounds on road – Squares M.17 at – 500 rounds fired at Hostile Aircraft. 1 am an aeroplane passed over Mill Post but could not be identified owing to darkness.	"
	25/1/17		Work restarted on Dugouts. 5:30pm – 9:30pm 2000 rounds fired on Sunken road M.15.d – M.27.a. 750 rounds fired at Hostile Aircraft.	"
	26/1/17		Work continued on Dug outs.	
	27/1/17		Relief of Gun teams carried out by day without incident.	
	28/1/17		Work continued on Dug outs. 5:30 – 10 pm 2750 rounds fired on road M.11.a.6.9 to M.5.d.4.1. and Trench M.16.d.9.5 to M.17.b.8.2. 250 rounds fired at Hostile Aeroplane.	
	29/1/17		Work continued on Dug outs. 6 pm – 10 pm 800 rounds searching Sunken road M.17.a.4.5. 250 rounds at Hostile Aeroplane. Tripods were mounted	
	30/1/17		Work continued on Dug outs. to fire on enemy front line in case of Road. barrage but none to fire. 1500 rounds were fired on road M.11.a.6.9. to M.5.d.4.1	
	31/1/17		Work continued on Dug outs. 1500 rounds at road and Trench M.16.d.9.5 to M.17 & 8.2 from 5:30 pm to 7 pm. 1500 rounds at Road and Dugt M.21.C.	

SBoughey Lt for Major
Comdg 42nd M.G. Coy

Vol 12

WAR DIARY

CONFIDENTIAL

UNIT 42nd Machine Gun Company

DATE From 1-2-17 to 28-2-17.

VOL NO XII

WAR DIARY
or
INTELLIGENCE SUMMARY

Army Form C. 2118.

HQ 2 Lochine Gun Coy

(Erase heading not required.)

Instructions regarding War Diaries and Intelligence Summaries are contained in F.S. Regs., Part II. and the Staff Manual respectively. Title pages will be prepared in manuscript.

Place	Date	Hour	Summary of Events and Information	Remarks and references to Appendices
Ly Sector 7th Corps Front	1/2/17		Work on Dugouts continued. 6.30pm – 11.30pm 2,250 rounds were fired at searching & road and light railway in M.17.a. 300 rounds fired at Hostile Aeroplane.	
	2/2/17		Work on Dugouts continued.	
	3/2/17		Relief of teams carried out by Day without incident.	
"	4/2/17		Work on Dugouts continued.	
"	5/2/17		Work on Dugouts continued. 6pm – 6.30pm 2000 rounds fired at DOMPS ROAD M.21.c. 500 rounds fired of hostile aeroplane. Work carried on Dugouts, arrangements set for reliefs of 21st & 89th Coys	Front line Dugouts Morters NEUVILLE VITASSE
"	6/2/17.		All guns of 62nd By except three retired to C. Echelon. Relieved by guns of 21st and 89th Coys. 82nd By less three guns moved into billets L.APPUS.	
"	8/2/17.		Six guns of 43rd By relieved by six guns of 42nd By, also two right lines taken over that same company. Five guns of 42nd By remaining in C.Echelon Relieved by three guns of 43rd By. 3500 rounds fired on several Harassing in M.6.d, J.16.c., & by night.	Front line Morters ARRAS
"	9/2/17		4000 rounds fired by night at various targets as on previous night.	
"	10/9/17		1150 rounds by night on Back Junctions H.6.C.M.S. between 7 Supp & 4pm	

Army Form C. 2118.

WAR DIARY
or
INTELLIGENCE SUMMARY.
(Erase heading not required.)

Army Form C. 2118.

20th Machine Gun Company

Instructions regarding War Diaries and Intelligence Summaries are contained in F.S. Regs., Part II. and the Staff Manual respectively. Title pages will be prepared in manuscript.

Place	Date	Hour	Summary of Events and Information	Remarks and references to Appendices
H. Sector VII Corps Front	11/2/17	7.30 p.m – 10 p.m	1250 rounds fired on BEAURAINS CROSS ROAD S.	
	12/2/17		Work delayed by fog in deepening HUNTER STREET. Two parties found for Brigade.	
"	13/2/17		Working party on HUNTER STREET shelled. Casualties 2/Lt. Dodd slightly wounded back. Two working parties found for Brigade.	
"	14/2/17		Work continued on HUNTER STREET by night. Two parties found for Brigade. Stove pipe fires by night on selected targets.	
"	15/2/17		Work continued on HUNTER STREET. Two other working parties found for Brigade. Teams relieved without incident.	
"	16/2/17		Work continued on HUNTER STREET. Site chosen for anti-aircraft gun. Fire opened by night traversing BEAURAINS – TILLOY ROAD and on BEAURAINS CROSS ROADS. Work continued on HUNTER STREET.	
"	17/2/17			
"	18/2/17		Work continued on HUNTER ST. Fire opened by two guns on selected targets by night.	

Army Form C. 2118.

WAR DIARY
or
INTELLIGENCE SUMMARY.
(Erase heading not required.)

Army Form C. 2118.

Hd.qrs Lachine Gun Coy

Place	Date	Hour	Summary of Events and Information	Remarks and references to Appendices
H Sector VII 6pto Fosse	19/2/17		Work continued at HUNTER STREET. Fire opened by night on M & L.G.S. when enemy working parties reported. A gun was reported to fire burst by day on this spot. Had 20 targets presented themselves. Within parties found for Brigade.	Plat 51/C Trench Map 1/10,000
"	20/2/17		Five Germans reported killed by fixed rifle fire for "Sniping Gun". One O.R. wounded on working party by Sgt N. Work continued at HUNTER STREET. Other parties fixed for Brigade. 1250 Rounds fired by sgt. at BEARAINS – NEUVILLE VITASSE ROAD.	
"	21/2/17		Five Germans hit by "Sniping" gun. Work continued at HUNTER STREET.	
"	22/2/17		Our Gunners reported hit by Sniping gun. Work continued at HUNTER STREET, other parties found for Brigade.	
"	23/2/17		Two victims claimed by sniping gun, two of these confirmed by other observers. Work continued at HUNTER STREET & other parties found for Brigade.	
"	24/2/17		Sniping Gun again active. Work continued at HUNTER STREET. Other parties found for Brigade.	
"	25/2/17		Sniping gun again claimed victims, 2nd & 3rd certified by other observers. Work continued at HUNTER STREET. Work started on two emplacements. Other parties found for Brigade.	

Army Form C. 2118.

WAR DIARY
or
INTELLIGENCE SUMMARY.

(Erase heading not required.)

Army No. 2 Machine Gun Company

Place	Date	Hour	Summary of Events and Information	Remarks and references to Appendices
Hunter Valleys Fort	26/8/17		Sniping gun active, several parties dispersed and one hits claimed. Both batteries on HUNTER STREET and 9 other parties seen for Brigade.	
"	27/8/17		Sniping gun active, also two anti-aircraft guns. Both retired on HUNTER STREET & other parties seen for Brigade. Fire opened by aps on enemy's back areas.	
"	28/8/17		Sniping gun active. Both retired on HUNTER STREET. Used as a new emplacement wherever.	

C.F. Fleewater Lieut.
O.C. No. 2 M.G. Cy

WAR DIARY.

CONFIDENTIAL.

UNIT. 42nd Machine Gun Coy.
T4

PERIOD. From 1-3-1917 to 31-3-1917

VOLUME NO. 13

Army Form C. 2118.

WAR DIARY
or
INTELLIGENCE SUMMARY.

(Erase heading not required.)

42nd Machine Gun Coy.

Instructions regarding War Diaries and Intelligence Summaries are contained in F.S. Regs., Part II. and the Staff Manual respectively. Title pages will be prepared in manuscript.

Place	Date	Hour	Summary of Events and Information	Remarks and references to Appendices
H. Ceeber VII Corps Front	1/3/17		Visibility fair. Claims three hits. Work carried on at HUNTER STREET. Other parties formed for Brigade. Teams in the line relieved without incident. Eff to enemy's air kept open at night.	
"	2/3/17		Similar gun active. Work continued at HUNTER STREET. Other parties formed for Brigade.	
"	3/3/17		Two guns relieved by 48th L.T.M. Bty. Work continued at HUNTER STREET. Other parties found by Brigade.	
"	4/3/17		Enemy's air early actively and 2 shoot hostile by Eff. Our shots continued at HUNTER STREET. Other parties found for Brigade.	
"	5/3/17		Effs to enemy's air kept open by Machine gun fire at night. Work continued at HUNTER STREET. Other working parties found for Brigade. Yso men to find at hostile aircraft.	
"	6/3/17		Hostile aeroplane brought back in enemy's lines by rifle, machine gun & Lewis gun fire. Work continued at HUNTER STREET. Other parties found for Brigade. Effs to enemy's air kept open by machine gun fire at night.	
"	7/3/17		Effs to enemy's air kept open by machine gun fire at night. Work carried on at HUNTER STREET. Other parties found for Brigade.	

Army Form C. 2118.

WAR DIARY
or
INTELLIGENCE SUMMARY

42nd M.G. Coy

(Erase heading not required.)

Place	Date	Hour	Summary of Events and Information	Remarks and references to Appendices
G Sector Village Font.	8/3/17		Work continued on HUNTER STREET. Other parties found for Brigade. Geps in wire kept open by night.	
	9/3/17		Work continued on HUNTER STREET. Other parties found for Brigade. Geps in wire kept open by night.	
	10/3/17		Geps in enemy's wire fired on by night. Other parties found for Brigade.	
	11/3/17		Geps in enemy's wire kept open during night. Work continued on HUNTER STREET and other parties found for Brigade. Relieving reconnaissance carried out to new front line.	
	12/3/17		Work continued on HUNTER STREET, other parties found for Brigade. Geps in enemy's wire fired on by night.	
	13/3/17		Geps in enemy's wire kept open by machine gun fire during the night. Work continued on HUNTER STREET & other parties found for Brigade.	
	14/3/17		Work continued on HUNTER STREET and other parties found for Brigade. Machine gun fire kept up by night on gaps in enemy's wire.	
	15/3/17		Two OR killed 6 OR wounded by shell fire on working party. Work continued on HUNTER STREET. Other parties found for Brigade. Geps in enemy's wire kept open during night.	

Army Form C. 2118.

WAR DIARY
or
INTELLIGENCE SUMMARY

(Erase heading not required.)

Army No. 42nd D.L.I.

Instructions regarding War Diaries and Intelligence Summaries are contained in F.S. Regs., Part II. and the Staff Manual respectively. Title pages will be prepared in manuscript.

Place	Date	Hour	Summary of Events and Information	Remarks and references to Appendices
H.Gelv. VII Cpl. S.O.I.	16/3/17		Work carried on HUNTER STREET; other parties found for Brigade. Gaps in enemy's wire kept open by a/n.	
"	17/3/17		Work carried on HUNTER STREET; other parties found for Brigade. Gaps in enemy's wire kept open during a/n. One Res. Gun post paraded to cover the a/n. J. Bryce fired by enforced pts in "No Man's Land" in case hostile raid.	
"	18/3/17	9.55a	S.O.S. signal seen opposite to be sent up from a/n. J. Bryce post, from which was put in the previous night to cover their a/n. fired 1760 rounds; another gun fired 750 or such; in SOS signal. Germans retired from their front system and in a/n. occupied by the left Coy of the line; flare recurring green sent up during the enemy to own line.	
"	19/3/17		Reconnaissance of new line; two new guns sent up to strengthen the position.	
"	20/3/17		Gun teams relieved without casualty. Gun post to old line withdrawn. 1 O.R. killed by shell fire.	
"	21/3/17		On our position sides and work continued or clearing old from a/n dug out.	
"	22/3/17		Reconnaissance of possible positions for large gins. Work carried on HUNTER STREET.	

Army Form C. 2118.

WAR DIARY
or
INTELLIGENCE SUMMARY

42nd M.G. Coy

(Erase heading not required.)

Instructions regarding War Diaries and Intelligence Summaries are contained in F. S. Regs. Part II. and the Staff Manual respectively. Title pages will be prepared in manuscript.

Place	Date	Hour	Summary of Events and Information	Remarks and references to Appendices
H Sector VII Corps Front	23/3/17		Further reconnaissance of barrage positions, took ordered at HUNTER STREET.	
	24/3/17		Company relieved by 91st Coy. Relief carried out by day without incident. Company moved back to billets in BERNEVILLE.	
BERNEVILLE	25/3/17		Refitting & repair.	
"	26/3/17		Training continued	
"	27/3/17		"	
"	28/3/17		"	
"	29/3/17		"	
"	30/3/17		"	
"	31/3/17		"	

W.S. Newburn Maj.
Comg 42nd M.G. Coy

War Diary

42nd Machine Gun Company

Vol. XIV

April 1917

WAR DIARY or INTELLIGENCE SUMMARY

Army Form C. 2118.

42nd Inf. Bde.

Place	Date	Hour	Summary of Events and Information	Remarks and references to Appendices
BERNEVILLE	1/4/17		Training continued.	
"	2/4/17		"	
"	3/4/17		"	
"	4/4/17		Seven guns moved into Atrecht to relieve guns of 21st Bde.	
"	5/4/17		Training continued BERNEVILLE.	
"	6/4/17		Remainder of by. moved up to the trenches and were accommodated in dugouts.	
# Lede	7/4/17		Preparations for offensive continued. Belt filling depots established and spare guns in readiness for filling.	
"	8/4/17		Preparations for offensive completed. Guns to be used for barrage fire and at dusk guns sent forward behind assembly troops ready to take up their positions in assembly trenches ready for fight.	
"	9/4/17		8 gns gunsfiring from ZERO – ZERO + 2 hours, six guns on the HARP and two on TILLOY, HARFLEUR & TRENCH a.s ZINX TRENCH to assist attack of Brigade on left + to engage any targets seen. Own to bad light no targets were seen. Seven guns were pushed behind the 5th + 7th Battalion this assembling in LADIES + LADIES Lane; four of these were to TELEGRAPH HILL to cover the right. Left to in detail to fulfil the capture of TELEGRAPH HILL final objective. Two teles.S to left Battalion allotted for capture of first objective. Casualties 1 officer (Fr. Lt. T. HAYES) and 2 in OR.	

WAR DIARY or INTELLIGENCE SUMMARY

Army Form C. 2118.

42nd D. of L.

Place	Date	Hour	Summary of Events and Information	Remarks and references to Appendices
H. Babs & trenches captured	9/4/17 (ctd.)		Wounded. No despatch provided themselves in any of those guns and no counter-attack developed to the front played by these guns and trench. Our teams were relieved during the afternoon.	
	10/4/17		Teams which were out relieved the previous day were relieved in the front trenches.	
	11/4/17		Other relieved during the evening.	
O.R. Acct.	12/4/17		By left reached H.2.a. at 2 Pavilion by 149th Bn being ready by left reached H.2.a. at 2 Pavilion to HAUTEVILLE supplying at DANVILLE for two days for breakfasts. Rifles and kilts at HAUTEVILLE about 2 pm. Orders received to march to AUBIGNY. Left marched off at 9.30 pm.	
		2.30 pm	2nd echelon into billets at 12.30 am 13th	
LIENCOURT	14/4/17		By Sevels to LIENCOURT.	
LE CAUROY.	15/4/17		By Sevels to LE CAUROY.	
	16/4/17		Training continued. 7 O.R. reinforcements joined.	
	17/4/17		Training continued so far as weather permitted.	
	18/4/17		" " " " — Reinforcement 1 of 23 OR joined.	
	19/4/17		Training continued.	
	20/4/17		Training continued.	
	21/4/17		Training continued. Musketeers of overhead fire carried out successfully.	

Army Form C. 2118.

WAR DIARY
or
INTELLIGENCE SUMMARY.

HQ 2 k G Bty

(Erase heading not required.)

Instructions regarding War Diaries and Intelligence Summaries are contained in F. S. Regs., Part II. and the Staff Manual respectively. Title pages will be prepared in manuscript.

Place	Date	Hour	Summary of Events and Information	Remarks and references to Appendices
BARLY LE CAUROY	22/4/17		Church Parade.	
BARLY	23/4/17		Bty marched to BARLY	
BELLACOURT – OLD GERMAN FRONT LINE.	24/4/17		Bty marched to BELLACOURT in the evening and became at old German front line in the evening.	
"	25/4/17		Bty relieved 151st Bty in trenches immediately south of COJEUL RIVER. 1 OR wounded.	
WANCOURT	26/4/17		Arrangements made for firing in cooperation with 15th Div. operations north of COJEUL RIVER.	
"	27/4/17	16.30	Fire opened on enemy trenches behind 9 buildings in OWL TRENCH.	
			15.a.5.15.	
"	28/4/17		Arrangements made for firing in cooperation with operations of 141st Bde. 5 guns relieved by right Sect of Bty. Bty relieved by right Sect of C 141st Bty in due course without incident.	Plus 5/13 Sqn
"	29/4/17		Preliminary reconnaissance for forthcoming operations. Bty relieved by right of C 141st Bde. Other teams	

Army Form C. 2118.

WAR DIARY
or
INTELLIGENCE SUMMARY

(Erase heading not required.)

H.Q. 2 b Bty.

Instructions regarding War Diaries and Intelligence Summaries are contained in F. S. Regs., Part II. and the Staff Manual respectively. Title pages will be prepared in manuscript.

Place	Date	Hour	Summary of Events and Information	Remarks and references to Appendices
Trenches near WANCOURT	30/4/17		Preliminary reconnaissance for forthcoming operations carried out. Preliminary wire cuts checked so to dispose of guns during operations discussed at Brigade Headquarters.	

L.P. Louden Maj.
By 2 b Bty.

CONFIDENTIAL

War Diary

42nd Machine Gun Company

1st–31st May 1917

Vol 15.

WAR DIARY
or
INTELLIGENCE SUMMARY
(Erase heading not required.)

Army Form C. 2118.

Place	Date	Hour	Summary of Events and Information	Remarks and references to Appendices
Trenches near WANCOURT	1/5/17		Preliminary arrangements for offensive continued.	
	2/5/17		Preliminary arrangements for offensive completed. 9 guns moved by night to positions as namely.	Sketch Ref V15-ENV-ARTDIS.
	3/5/17		All Gers guns were shortstops as follows. Four guns in APE TRENCH, two guns in BUCK TRENCH, two guns in QUARRY at the N end of BOAR TRENCH, two guns in BANK in rear of BOAR TRENCH about O.186.9.4., 4 guns in Brigade Reserve in PANTHER TRENCH. At Zero (3.45 a.m.) to no of the guns in Piccany opened fire in STROHART FACTORY to cover advance of 56th Div on the left. 4 guns opened up fire until Z+40 hours when both guns harassed forward eastwards of Ohio. At the same time the guns per APE TRENCH moved forward. As the objectives were not taken the guns eventually returned to APE TRENCH. Four guns were also to fire on German parry covered in church Brigade Reserve front ever Essex facing the bay. They stood to down to two to cover the COVER VALLEY. Casualties 3 OR killed, 2 officers 17 OR wounded.	

A8534. Wt.W4973/M687 750,000 8/16 D. D. & L. Ltd. Forms/C.2118/13

Army Form C. 2118.

WAR DIARY
or
INTELLIGENCE SUMMARY.
(Erase heading not required.)

Instructions regarding War Diaries and Intelligence Summaries are contained in F. S. Regs., Part II. and the Staff Manual respectively. Title pages will be prepared in manuscript.

Place	Date	Hour	Summary of Events and Information	Remarks and references to Appendices
Maroeuil area	2/5/17		Bn relieved by 4 D. Coy.	
WANCOURT THE HARP	5/4/17		Bn reached THE HARP.	
"	6/5/17		Nothing to report.	
"	7/5/17		6 O.R. joined as reinforcements.	
"	8/5/17		Nothing to report	
"	9/5/17		"	
"	10/5/17		"	
"	11/5/17		"	
"	12/5/17		"	
"	13/5/17		"	
"	14/5/17		Working party fired on by Bojah. 3 O.R. wounded.	
"	15/5/17		" " " " " " 1 O.R. wounded.	
Sepport huts	16/5/17		Bn moved into Sepport area.	
"	17/5/17		Bn began work at Rifle Range for Brigade.	

WAR DIARY
or
INTELLIGENCE SUMMARY.
(Erase heading not required.)

Army Form C. 2118.

Place	Date	Hour	Summary of Events and Information	Remarks and references to Appendices
Sefford Huts	18/5/17		Bn marched to Rifle Range.	
"	19/5/17		Bn marched to Rifle Range. Reconnaissance of ground made by Officers & NCOs.	
"	20/5/17		Bn continued on Rifle Range.	
"	21/5/17		Rifle Range completed.	
"	22/5/17		Nothing to report.	
"	23/5/17		Final tests & instruction given to attached men on Ranges.	
Trenches Lefroy Sap	24/5/17		Bn relieved 11 Lt By in the trenches. 2 OR killed. 10 OR wounded. Officers 2/Lt P. Huffy gassed.	
"	25/5/17		One gun withdrawn from the line.	
"	26/5/17		Enemy prisoners raid near HARCOURT. 10R killed 1 OR wounded. two from enemy enemy strong-post. Two German officers taken.	

WAR DIARY or INTELLIGENCE SUMMARY.

Army Form C. 2118.

(Erase heading not required.)

Instructions regarding War Diaries and Intelligence Summaries are contained in F. S. Regs., Part II. and the Staff Manual respectively. Title pages will be prepared in manuscript.

Place	Date	Hour	Summary of Events and Information	Remarks and references to Appendices
Trenches 24th Div. G.P.O. Front	27/5/17		1 OR wounded from the line. 1 Pioneer slightly shelled. 2 OR slightly wounded at Artois Camp.	
	28/5/17		2 OR slightly wounded at Artois Camp.	
	29/5/17		1 OR killed, 2 OR wounded. Shrap. Gun. 1st Coy v Epinn 43rd Coy came into the line relieved by first teams aircraft operation.	
	30/5/17		Q. firing was done at hostile aircraft owing to the fact that our men were opposed with Lewis gun. 2 OR missing from relief carrying our fire work to a new position entering the cover valley + running to certain Infm action accused from a pillbox coffered by us kept the in effect that an attack took place of the River had been widened the previous night. Two OR looking at 30 h. injured showing they they way the previous night.	

Sgd S Phelan Lay.
Lay U.S. 2 R.M. Reg.

Vol 16

War Diary.
42ᵈ Machine Gun Company.
Vol. XVI.
June 1917

Army Form C. 2118.

WAR DIARY
or
INTELLIGENCE SUMMARY.
(Erase heading not required.)

Instructions regarding War Diaries and Intelligence Summaries are contained in F.S. Regs., Part II. and the Staff Manual respectively. Title pages will be prepared in manuscript.

42nd Machine Gun Company

Place	Date	Hour	Summary of Events and Information	Remarks and references to Appendices
Trenches Left of VII Corps Front	1/6/17	10.45pm - 2.15am	4000 rounds fired on Sunken Road at N.32.a.7.3 by 2 guns in Enfilade.	Ref. VIS EN ARTOIS 1/10000
	2/6/17	5.30am	150 rounds fired at hostile aeroplane approaching. It turned & went back.	
	3/6/17		Relieved in line without incident by 43rd M.G. Coy. Relief Complete 11.45 am. Moved into Support Area.	
BEAURAINS	4/6/17		Moved into Divisional reserve near BEAURAINS.	
	5/6/17		Commenced Training	
	6/6/17		Training Continued	
	7/6/17		" "	
	8/6/17		Two guns attached to 47th Bde R.F.A. relieved and rejoined Coy.	
BEAUMETZ	9/6/17		Marched to BEAUMETZ. Arrived in Billets 9.30 am. No men fell out.	
SAULTY	10/6/17		Marched to SAULTY. Arrived in Billets 9.45 am. No men fell out.	
BEAUQUESNE	11/6/17		Marched to BEAUQUESNE. Arrived in Billets 11 am. 2 men fell out. Axle of one of the rear limbers broke. Was left behind and sent for next day.	
"	12/6/17		Commenced Training	
"	13/6/17		Training Continued	
"	14/6/17		Training Continued	
"	15/6/17		Training Continued	

Army Form C. 2118.

WAR DIARY
or
INTELLIGENCE SUMMARY.
42º Machine Gun Company

(Erase heading not required.)

Place	Date	Hour	Summary of Events and Information	Remarks and references to Appendices
BEAUQUESNE	16/6/17		Training continued	
"	17/6/17		Church Parade.	
"	18/6/17		Training continued	
"	19/6/17		Company paraded thro' gas chamber to test fitting of box respirators. Training continued.	
"	20/6/17		Training continued. Eliminating trials for 2 of Company commenced.	
"	21/6/17		Training continued. Eliminating trials for 2 of Company continued. 2/Lt E. Lamb & 30R joined as reinforcements.	
"	22/6/17		Traction gun competition. Training continued.	
"	23/6/17		Training continued.	
"	24/6/17		Church Parade	
"	25/6/17		Training continued.	
"	26/6/17		Training continued.	
"	27/6/17		Training continued.	
"	28/6/17		Training continued.	

Army Form C. 2118.

WAR DIARY
or
INTELLIGENCE SUMMARY. 42º Lucknow Jean Coy.
(Erase heading not required.)

Place	Date	Hour	Summary of Events and Information	Remarks and references to Appendices
BEAUSOESNE	29/6/17		Training continued. One section carried out field firing with 9th Rifle Brigade.	
"	30/6/17		Training continued.	

G.Y. Meader Lieut.
Comdg 42º O L &. Coy

CONFIDENTIAL

WAR DIARY.

Vol 17

UNIT   42nd. Machine Gun Coy.

PERIOD   1st to 31st July 1917.

VOLUME No 17.

Army Form C. 2118.

WAR DIARY
or
INTELLIGENCE SUMMARY.
(Erase heading not required.)

Instructions regarding War Diaries and Intelligence Summaries are contained in F.S. Regs., Part II. and the Staff Manual respectively. Title pages will be prepared in manuscript.

Place	Date	Hour	Summary of Events and Information	Remarks and references to Appendices
BEAUQUESNE	1/7/17		Church Parade.	
"	2/7/17		Training continued. Sector field firing with 9th Rifle Brigade.	
"	3/7/17		Training continued. Sector field firing with 9th K.R.R.C.	
"	4/7/17		Training continued.	
"	5/7/17		Training continued. On sector field firing with 5th Oxf&Bucks L.I. & shafts.	
"	6/7/17		Training continued. On sector field firing with 5th K.S.L.I.	
"	7/7/17		Training continued. On sector field firing with 5th K.S.L.I.	
"	8/7/17		Church Parade	
"	9/7/17		Training continued.	
"	10/7/17		Training continued.	
"	11/7/17		Company marched to CANDAS and entrained to BAILLEUL	
BAILLEUL	12/7/17		Company detrained at BAILLEUL, enemy aeroplane dropped bombs near shelter during detrainment. Casualties nil. Company arrived in camp 4 a.m.	
"	14/7/17		Training continued, reconnaisance of route to WYTSCHAETE carried out. Lt WILLSON and 2nd Lt PRICE joined company.	

A 5834 Wt W4973/M687 750,000 8/16 D. D. & L. Ltd. Forms/C.2118/13.

Army Form C. 2118.

WAR DIARY
or
INTELLIGENCE SUMMARY.
(Erase heading not required.)

Instructions regarding War Diaries and Intelligence Summaries are contained in F.S. Regs., Part II. and the Staff Manual respectively. Title pages will be prepared in manuscript.

Place	Date	Hour	Summary of Events and Information	Remarks and references to Appendices
BAILLEOL	14/7/17		Training continued	
"	15/7/17		Church Parade. Inspection and 2nd TRENT DUMP or AA duty.	
"	16/7/17		Training continued.	
"	17/7/17		Training continued; reconnaissance of Coys etc.	
"	18/7/17		Training continued.	
"	19/7/17		Training continued	
"	20/7/17		Training continued.	
"	21/7/17		Training Continued	
"	22/7/17		Church Parade.	
"	23/7/17		New line reconnoitred	
"	24/7/17		Training Continued	
"	25/7/17		Training Continued	
"	26/7/17		Training Continued	
"	27/7/17		Training Continued Two guns on AA duty at TRENT DUMP relieved by 249th M.G. Coy	
"	28/7/17		Training Continued	
"	29/7/17		Church Parade cancelled owing to Rain	
"	30/7/17		Training Continued	
"	31/7/17		Preparations complete for Move	

S Romphrey a/Capt
Comdg 242nd M.G. Coy

WAR DIARY

42nd Machine Gun Company

Volume XVIII   August 1917

Army Form C. 2118.

WAR DIARY
or
INTELLIGENCE SUMMARY.
(Erase heading not required.)

Instructions regarding War Diaries and Intelligence
Summaries are contained in F. S. Regs., Part II.
and the Staff Manual respectively. Title pages
will be prepared in manuscript.

Place	Date	Hour	Summary of Events and Information	Remarks and references to Appendices
Bailleul	1/8/17		Stood to. Ready to move at one hours notice till 11 am	
	2/8/17		Training Continued	
	3/8/17		Training Continued } much interfered with by Rain	
	4/8/17		Training Continued	
	5/8/17		Training Continued (Church Parade)	
	6/8/17		Marched from Bailleul to Pradelles	
Pradelles	7/8/17		Training Continued	
	8/8/17		Training Continued	
	9/8/17		Training Continued	
	10/8/17		Training Continued	
	11/8/17		Training Continued	
	12/8/17		Church Parade.	
	13/8/17		Training Continued	
	14/8/17		Training Continued	
	15/8/17		Training Continued	
OUDEDOM	16/8/17		Moved by Bus to Oudedom Area. Lecture by II Corps Intelligence Officer on ground in front of 42nd Infde line. Also visited model of ground.	
DICKEBUSCH	17/8/17		Moved to Transport Camp near DICKEBUSCH.	
	18/8/17		Reconnoitred line occupied by 58th Div between WESTHOEK and MENIN ROAD. In evening relieved 4 guns of 167th M.G. Coy, 5 guns of 168 M.G.Coy + 2 guns of 169 m.g. Coy. Relief completed 9.40 pm without incident.	
TRENCHES before GLENCORSE WOOD	19/8/17		4 guns on WESTHOEK RIDGE fairly heavily shelled. 2 OR killed 2 OR wounded.	

A5834 Wt. W4973/M687 750,000 8/16 D. D. & L. Ltd Forms/C.2118/13.

WAR DIARY or INTELLIGENCE SUMMARY

(Erase heading not required.)

Army Form C. 2118.

Place	Date	Hour	Summary of Events and Information	Remarks and references to Appendices
TRENCHES before GLENCORSE WOOD	20/8/17		Preparations for offensive. 1 OR wounded (gas) near Halfway House.	
	21/8/17		Preparation for offensive.	
	22/8/17		7500 rounds fired in Divisional Barrage from CHATEAU WOOD on to T.15.c.3.7½ and northwards for 200 yds by 4 guns to assist in 14th Divl Operations. 6000 rounds fired from 4 guns on Westhoek Ridge on to Western Edge of Polygon Wood in response to SOS signal from Front Line. 2 guns from Tunnel T.13.b.8.50 moved forward with 5th KSLI into GLENCORSE WOOD. One gun put out of action. 2 guns got forward into positions (1) in Jargon Trench (2) about T.14.a.8.5. Latter gun received several targets. 5th KSLI in establishing forward posts. Both guns sent 2 more guns moved forward about dawn to take up defensive positions behind. 1 Officer killed, 1 OR killed, 7 OR wounded, 1 OR missing. 1 Officer wounded + missing, 10 R missing.	
	23/8/17		6 guns teams relieved by Reserve personnel from Coy Hqrs. Enemy Counterattack on Brigade on Right gun at T.14.a.8.5 got several targets. 2 guns on Westhoek Ridge. 2 guns in Chateau Wood relieved during evening by 142nd MG Coy. 6 OR wounded.	
	24/8/17		Nothing to report during day. 2 guns on Westhoek ridge relieved by 142nd MG Coy. Relief of remaining 6 guns by 70th MG Coy started.	
	25/8/17		Relief completed 7.30 am. 2 OR wounded. Company moved back to WIPPENHOEK Area.	
WIPPENHOEK AREA	26/8/17 27/8/17 28/8/17 29/8/17		Inspections + Cleaning up.	
THIUSHOEK AREA	30/8/17 31/8/17		Moved to THIUSHOEK AREA. Training commenced. Training continued.	

S Rowntree? / Capt
Comdg 42nd MG Coy

Vol 19

WAR DIARY

42nd MACHINE GUN COMPANY

Volume XIX   September 1917

Army Form C. 2118.

WAR DIARY
or
INTELLIGENCE SUMMARY.
(Erase heading not required.)

Instructions regarding War Diaries and Intelligence Summaries are contained in F.S. Regs., Part II. and the Staff Manual respectively. Title pages will be prepared in manuscript.

Place	Date	Hour	Summary of Events and Information	Remarks and references to Appendices
Neuve Eglise Area	1/9/17		Moved to NEUVE EGLISE area (Hillside Camp) Party went forward to reconnoitre line East of MESSINES. Transport and Details took over Transport Camp T.9d. Caution from 90th M.G. Coy.	Ref Belgium & France Sheet 28.
"	2/9/17			"
Trenches East of MESSINES	3/9/17		On night of 2nd/3rd Company relieved 16 guns of 90th M.G. Coy in line from O.35 to U.1.b. approx. 1 gun destroyed by direct shell, 4 ORs killed about 1am on night of 3rd/4th. 16 guns relieved by 6 guns of 249th M.G. Coy. Line reconnoitred with 2M.G.O. with a view to rearrangement of M.G's.	"
"	4/9/17			"
"	5/9/17		Moved up new gun to position at SEPTIEME BARN to cover Reserve line Southwards and changed 1 gun from Borrow position to new position U.11.a.7.9 to cover windmill (U.5.b.80)	"
"	6/9/17		Line reconnoitred with Bde Major + 2M.G.O.	"
"	7/9/17		On night 6th/7th Teams of Coy – line relieved by fresh teams from Details Camp. 2 Officers + 2 ORs wounded. 1 OR killed.	"
"	8/9/17		2 guns moved up to Steignast Farm (one firing northwards and one Southwards to cover support line). 1 gun moved to YAPARD firing south to cover Support line. One gun moved up to SEPTIEME BARN to cover Reserve line Northwards and 1 gun to O.34.b.2.3 to cover valley of BLAUWEPOORTBEEK.	"
"	9/9/17		Nothing to report.	"
"	10/9/17		Night of 10/11th Coy relieved by 40th M.G. Coy and went back to Camp T.9.d. Central.	"
"	11/9/17		Commenced Training.	"
"	12/9/17			"
Neuve Eglise Area	13/9/17		Company provided Working Party of 100 men on Mule Truck.	"
"	14/9/17		Training continued. Working Party of 46 provided.	"
"	15/9/17		Marched to BERQUIN Area in Reserve to 57th Div.	"
BERQUIN AREA	16/9/17		Training Continued	

Army Form C. 2118.

WAR DIARY
or
INTELLIGENCE SUMMARY.
(Erase heading not required.)

Instructions regarding War Diaries and Intelligence Summaries are contained in F.S. Regs., Part II. and the Staff Manual respectively. Title pages will be prepared in manuscript.

Place	Date	Hour	Summary of Events and Information	Remarks and references to Appendices
RERQUIN AREA	17/9/17		Training Continued	Ref Belgium & France Sheet 28
	18/9/17		Marched to Camp at T 27 a 4 5	
NEUVE EGLISE AREA	19/9/17		Training Continued	
"	20/9/17		Training Continued	
"	21/9/17		Training Continued	
"	22/9/17		Training Continued. Reconnoitred Valley West of MESSINES with 2nd M.G.O. to select Anti aircraft positions to protect the Batteries (Field) from low flying aircraft. These 4 guns moved up at night and occupied positions (1) Hell Wood (2) O 32 6-10. 20, 13) Near Gooseberry Farm (3) U.13 a 7 6.7 6.	
"	23/9/17		Training Continued. 1500 rounds fired at Hostile Aircraft	
"	24/9/17		Training Continued. 1000 rounds fired at Hostile Aircraft.	
"	25/9/17		Training Continued 950 rounds at Hostile Aircraft.	
"	26/9/17		Training Continued 1000 rounds at Hostile Aircraft.	
"	27/9/17		Training Continued.	
"	28/9/17		Relieved 9 guns of 43rd M.G.Coy in line and also 2 guns of 249th M.G. Coy in line. Very good relief. Complete by 10 p.m. 4 guns on Anti aircraft work relieved by 4th M.G. Coy.	
"	29/9/17		Nothing to report. Two concrete dugouts cleared of water & dirt with a view to their being used for Machine guns.	
"	30/9/17		Nothing further to report.	

S Roumphrey a/Capt
Comdg.
42nd Machine Gun Company.

WAR DIARY

42nd MACHINE GUN COMPANY

OCTOBER 1917

VOLUME XX

WAR DIARY or INTELLIGENCE SUMMARY

Army Form C. 2118.

(Erase heading not required.)

Place	Date	Hour	Summary of Events and Information	Remarks and references to Appendices
Trenches East of MESSINES	1/10/17		Found Antiaircraft Positions for Nos 7 + 8 Guns.	Ref Religious France Sheet 28
	2/10/17		Found Antiaircraft Positions for Nos 9 + 10 Guns.	
	3/10/17		Moved No 16 Gun to Pill Box at U.4.6.22. Covering Steignast Farm to Right. 3000 rounds fired at Hostile Aircraft.	
	4/10/17		750 rounds fired at Hostile Aircraft.	
	5/10/17		1200 rounds fired at Hostile Aircraft. 2750 rounds at Esperance Cuts and tracks round it at intervals during night of 4th/5th.	
	6/10/17		1500 rounds fired at Hostile Aircraft.	
	7/10/17		700 rounds fired at Hostile Aircraft. OC 19th MG Coy reconnoitred line and arranged details of relief.	
	8/10/17		Relieved by 19th M.G. Coy. Fairly difficult relief.	
NEUVE EGLISE	9/10/17		Nothing to report.	
	10/10/17		Marched to THIEUSHOOK.	
THIEUSHOOK	11/10/17		Marched to RIDGE WOOD. Divisional Reserve.	
RIDGE WOOD	12/10/17		Nothing to report.	
	13/10/17		Nothing to report.	
	14/10/17		Went to 41st MG Coy Pole Hope Top Top. to arrange for relief of 41st MG Coy.	
	15/10/17		Preparations for line.	
	16/10/17		Preparations for line. Moved from present Camp to Dotrils Camp.	
	17/10/17		Relieved 41st MG Coy in line before POLDERHOEK CHATEAU. Very good relief with only 1 OR wounded.	
TRENCHES West of POLDERHOEK CHATEAU	18/10/17		1 Gun in Suffolt line destroyed by direct hit. 3 ORs wounded. 1 NYDN case. Reserve Section Hqrs moved and improved accommodation of teams.	

WAR DIARY
or
INTELLIGENCE SUMMARY.
(Erase heading not required.)

Army Form C. 2118.

Instructions regarding War Diaries and Intelligence Summaries are contained in F. S. Regs., Part II and the Staff Manual respectively. Title pages will be prepared in manuscript.

Place	Date	Hour	Summary of Events and Information	Remarks and references to Appendices
Trenches West of POLDERHOEK CHATEAU	19/10/17 20/10/17		Nothing to report except naval shelling. 1 Bomb dropped on Transport Camp, killing 1 OR & wounding 5 ORs. also 1 Horse + 1 Mule wounded. Reconnoitred positions for front lined guns to work with draw to on morning of 22nd during evacuation of front line while leaves. Bombarded POLDERHOEK CHATEAU. Trench boards carried up and E track maintained between PLUMERS DRIVE + STIRLING CASTLE. 850 rounds at Hostile Aircraft.	
	21/10/17		Ammunition carried up to Barrage positions. Arrangements made for relief by 13th M.G. Coy. 750 rounds at Hostile Aircraft.	
	22/10/17		Guns from front line withdrawn to positions near NORTHAMPTON FARM during day. 2 ORs killed + 7 ORs wounded. More ammunition carried up to Barrage Positions. 1200 rounds at Hostile Aircraft.	
	23/10/17		6 Guns relieved by 13th M.G. Coy. 1 OR killed.	
	24/10/17		Rest Remaining 6 Guns relieved by 204th M.G. Coy. 1 OR wounded. Company moved by march and lorry to THIEUSHOOK.	
THIEUSHOOK	25/10/17		Cleaning up etc	
	26/10/17		Inspections etc	
	27/10/17		Training Commenced.	
	28/10/17		Training Continued	
	29/10/17		Training Continued	
	30/10/17		Training Continued	
	31/10/17		Training Continued 23 ORs reinforcements reported for duty	

Vol 21

Confidential

War Diary

42nd Machine Gun Coy.

1st to 30th November 1917.

Volumn No 21.

WAR DIARY or INTELLIGENCE SUMMARY.

Army Form C. 2118.

(Erase heading not required.)

Instructions regarding War Diaries and Intelligence Summaries are contained in F.S. Regs., Part II. and the Staff Manual respectively. Title pages will be prepared in manuscript.

Place	Date	Hour	Summary of Events and Information	Remarks and references to Appendices
THIEUSHOUK	1/11/17	—	Training Continued.	
"	2/11/17		Training Continued.	
"	3/11/17		Training Continued.	
"	4/11/17		Training Continued.	
"	5/11/17		Training Continued.	
"	6/11/17		Training Continued.	
"	7/11/17		Training Continued.	
"	8/11/17		Training Continued.	
"	9/11/17		Training Continued.	
"	10/11/17		Training Continued.	
"	11/11/17		Training Continued.	
"	12/11/17		Company entrained. Transport & loading party at BAILLEUL. Remainder of Coy at CAESTRE detrained at WIZERNES and marched to very good billets at WESTBECOURT.	
WESTBECOURT	13/11/17		Cleaning up etc. Training area reconnoitred.	
"	14/11/17		Training Commenced	
"	15/11/17		Training Continued	
"	16/11/17		Training Continued	
"	17/11/17		Training Continued	
"	18/11/17		Training Continued	
"	19/11/17		Training Continued	
"	20/11/17		Training Continued	
"	21/11/17		Training Continued	

Army Form C. 2118.

WAR DIARY
or
INTELLIGENCE SUMMARY.
(Erase heading not required.)

Instructions regarding War Diaries and Intelligence Summaries are contained in F. S. Regs., Part II. and the Staff Manual respectively. Title pages will be prepared in manuscript.

Place	Date	Hour	Summary of Events and Information	Remarks and references to Appendices
WESTBECOURT	22/11/17		Training Continued	
"	23/11/17		Training Continued	
"	24/11/17		Training Continued	
"	25/11/17		Training Continued	
"	26/11/17		Training Continued	
"	27/11/17		Training Continued	
"	28/11/17		Training Continued	
"	29/11/17		Transport moved from WESTBECOURT to HALLINES.	
"	30/11/17		Company entrained at WIZERNES and detrained at BRANDHOEK.	

S Humphrey / Capt
Co.dg 42nd M.G. Coy

War Diary

42nd Machine Gun Coy.

December 1917.

Volumn 22.

Army Form C. 2118.

WAR DIARY

or

~~INTELLIGENCE SUMMARY.~~

(Erase heading not required.)

Instructions regarding War Diaries and Intelligence Summaries are contained in F.S. Regs., Part II. and the Staff Manual respectively. Title pages will be prepared in manuscript.

Place	Date	Hour	Summary of Events and Information	Remarks and references to Appendices
BRANDHOEK	1/12/17		Moved into huts near Cross Roads.	
"	2/12/17		Moved into Camp at ST JEAN and made arrangements for relief of 25th M.G. Coy	
"	3/12/17		Relieved 12 guns of 25th M.G. Coy in Barrage positions near CREST FARM in the PASCHENDAELE Sector. 1 O.R. killed. 1 O.R. wounded.	
TRENCHES	4/12/17		Nothing to report	
"	5/12/17		2 guns moved up from details to occupy positions near KOREK to defend Corps line.	
"	6/12/17		Inter Company relief without incident	
"	7/12/17		Nothing to report	
"	8/12/17		Nothing to report	
"	9/12/17		Company relieved by guns of 224th M.G. Coy and proceeded to Camp at ST JEAN.	
ST JEAN	10/12/17		Cleaned up.	
"	11/12/17		Nothing to report	
"	12/12/17		Nothing to report	
"	13/12/17		Nothing to report	
"	14/12/17		Preparing for line	
TRENCHES	15/12/17		Relieved 15 guns of 224th M.G. Coy in line. 12 in Barrage Position. 2 at KOREK, 1 at WURST FARM. 1 Officer, 1 O.R. buried (wounded)	
"	16/12/17		Nothing to report	
"	17/12/17		Nothing to report	
"	18/12/17		Inter Company relief without incident.	
"	19/12/17		Nothing to report.	
"	20/12/17		2 guns moved from present to new Barrage Positions D.4.b.20.22. & D.4.b.20.23. 20,000 rounds S.A.A. also carried up to them from Details Camp.	Sheet 28.

Army Form C. 2118.

WAR DIARY
~~INTELLIGENCE SUMMARY~~

(Erase heading not required.)

Place	Date	Hour	Summary of Events and Information	Remarks and references to Appendices
TRENCHES	21/12/17		Company relieved by 224th M.G. Coy and proceeded to Camp at BRANDHOEK.	
BRANDHOEK	22/12/17		Cleaning up etc.	
"	23/12/17		Preparations for move. Advance party sent to TILQUES Area.	
"	24/12/17		" " " Transport moved to WORMHOUDT.	
"	25/12/17		Coy entrained at BRANDHOEK & detrained at WIZERNES, thence marching to TATINGHEM.	
TATINGHEM	26/12/17		Cleaning up etc.	
"	27/12/17		" "	
"	28/12/17		Training Commenced	
"	29/12/17		" continued.	
"	30/12/17		Nothing to Report. Billeting Officers sent on in advance to new Area.	
"	31/12/17		Operation Orders for move of Brigade to SUZANNE area received. Preparations for move.	

J. M. Sharing Lieut
for O.C. 142nd M.G. Coy.

Vol 23

War Diary

42nd Machine Gun Coy.

January 1918.

Volumn 23.

WAR DIARY
INTELLIGENCE SUMMARY

Army Form C. 2118.

Place	Date	Hour	Summary of Events and Information	Remarks and references to Appendices
TATINGHEM	1/1/18		Coy entrained at ST OMER for SUZANNE. Good journey. Detrained at ERQUHILL (near) arriving in huts at 1 AM.	
SUZANNE	2/1/18		Cleaning up.	
"	3/1/18		" "	
"	4/1/18		Training commenced.	
"	5/1/18		" continued.	
"	6/1/18		Church Parade.	
"	7/1/18		Court of Enquiry on Hut destroyed by fire at BRANDHOEK. Training continued.	
"	8/1/18		Training continued.	
"	9/1/18		Training continued.	
"	10/1/18		" "	
"	11/1/18		" "	
"	12/1/18		" "	
"	13/1/18		Church Parade.	
"	14/1/18		Training continued.	
"	15/1/18		" "	
"	16/1/18		" "	
"	17/1/18		" "	
"	18/1/18		" " Transport inspected by G.O.C. 42nd Inf. Bde.	

Army Form C. 2118.

WAR DIARY
or
INTELLIGENCE SUMMARY.
(Erase heading not required.)

Instructions regarding War Diaries and Intelligence Summaries are contained in F. S. Regs., Part II. and the Staff Manual respectively. Title pages will be prepared in manuscript.

Place	Date	Hour	Summary of Events and Information	Remarks and references to Appendices
SUZANNE	19/1/18		Training continued. Lecture by Courts Martial expert. Inter Section Competition for Silver Cup presented by C.O.C. 42nd INF. BDE.	
"	20/1/18		Preparations for move. Billeting Officer sent to new area.	
"	21/1/18		Coy marched to VRELY, distance of 15 miles. No one fell out. Billeting Officer sent to new area.	
VRELY	22/1/18		Coy marched to SAULEHOY-SUR-DAVENSCOURT. Distance 10 miles. No one fell out.	
SAULEHOY	23/1/18		Cleaning up etc. Transport moved to CANNOR under Bde arrangements.	
"	24/1/18		One Officer sent forward to reconnoitre new line & make arrangements for Relief. Coy marched to ERCHES for emtraining. Arrived at BERLANCOURT & marched to BEINES. Transport moved from CANNOR to BEINES.	
BEINES	25/1/18			
MONTESCOURT	26/1/18		Coy marched to MONTESCOURT to Details Camp.	
"	27/1/18		Preparations for the line.	
Trenches about 6 miles South of ST QUENTIN.	28/1/18		Ten guns taken over from the FRENCH. Very easy Relief. Relief completed 9 P.M.	
"	29/1/18		Line reconnoitred with a view to improvement.	
"	30/1/18		One gun moved to new position at H.5.d.90.10. Firing N.E. down ravine through BOIS D'URVILLERS 500 yds at north aircraft.	
"	31/1/18		Further reconnaissance of the line. Several anti-aircraft emplacements built.	

D Bomphrey a/Capt
cmdg 42nd M.G. Coy

Vol 24

War Diary

42nd Machine Gun Company

February 1918.

Volumn 24.

Army Form C. 2118.

Instructions regarding War Diaries and Intelligence Summaries are contained in F. S. Regs., Part II. and the Staff Manual respectively. Title pages will be prepared in manuscript.

WAR DIARY
INTELLIGENCE SUMMARY.
(Erase heading not required.)

Place	Date	Hour	Summary of Events and Information	Remarks and references to Appendices
TRENCHES	1/2/18	—	PECHINE TRENCH area reconnoitred for gun positions covering VALLÉE -AUX- CORBEAUX.	Aφ: FRANCE 66 C.N.W.
"	2/2/18	—	Liaison arranged between H12 M.G. Coy.	
"	3/2/18	—	Conference with D.M.G.O. New line between BOIS-DE-LAMBAY & MANUFACTURE F.M. reconnoitred. One gun moved to H6 C 30-30 to give NORTH WARDS in front of PECHINE TRENCH. 3900 rds fired at hostile aircraft.	
"	4/2/18	—	6 gun teams - ammunition etc. moved to Bde: H.q. to be in readiness to man line of resistance. Further reconnaissance of this line.	
"	5/2/18	—	Line reconnoitred with D.M.G.O.	
"	6/2/18	—	ESSIGNY – BENAY line reconnoitred.	
"	7/2/18	—	ESSIGNY – BENAY LINE reconnoitred with tel: connecty 42nd Inf: Bde. with a view to cooperation with 224th M.G. Coy.	
"	8/2/18	—	ESSIGNY – BENAY LINE reconnoitred with O.C. 14th Aux: M.G. Battn.	
"	9/2/18	—	Alternative position to cover valley in front of Right Battn 42nd Inf: Bde. blown up. Activy. Complete by 11-15 P.M. without incident. 2,500 rds fired at hostile aircraft.	
"	10/2/18	—	Reconnoitred the ESSIGNY – BENAY LINE to improve defence of BOIS – de – LAMBAY. Position to fire on H12 Inf: Bde Front found at about H6 a 90-10. 100 rds at hostile aircraft.	
"	11/2/18	—	The Forward Zone visited with the Battn Commander with a view to M.G. Defence.	
"	12/2/18	—	One gun of H12 M.G. Coy returned one gun of H2 M.G. Coy at H5 b 5.5. This gun was then moved to new position at H6 a 9.5.10 to cover front of H12 Inf: Bde. Work started on dugout at this position.	

Army Form C. 2118.

WAR DIARY
or
INTELLIGENCE SUMMARY.
(Erase heading not required.)

Place	Date	Hour	Summary of Events and Information	Remarks and references to Appendices
TRENCHES	12.2.18 cont:		One gun from H.qr. moved to new position at H.4.d.60.80. to cover Valley NORTH of B'DURVILLERS	
"	13.2.18		Two guns in the Battle Zone near LA SABLIERE relieved by 412th M.G. Coy. Left gun of 224th M.G. Coy. in front of LANBAY WOOD taken over. M.G. Coy in front of LANBAY WOOD taken over	
"	14.2.18		From 8 P.M. to 12.30 am 3000 rds were fired at Enemy Battn: H.qr. ─ road & Trench T tramway & road junction at approx. B.25.t.80.89.	
"	15.2.18		1500 rounds fired by our M.g's on Bn Hqrs at J.2.b.30.30 from 6p to 12 (midnight). 3000 rounds at Hostile Aircraft	
"	16.2.18		Our M.g's fired 2000 rounds on tracks at J.2.b.90.05 from 6.15p.─11p. 900 rounds at gun of 42nd M.G. Coy at H.5.t.45.75 Hostile Aircraft.	
"	17.2.18		Gun of 42nd M.G Coy at H.5.t.45.75 changed places with gun of 412th M.G. Coy. H.5.t.45.50.	
"	18.2.18.		Our M.g's fired as follows. (a) 1500 rounds on tracks in J.3.t.70.05. (b.) 1000 rounds on Cross Roads J.8.c.40.65. (c) 1000 rounds at J.14.a.55.75. Coy Hqrs & Track. between	
"	19.2.18		6p─10.30p─ 750 rounds fired on tracks at J.8.C.40.65. and 1000 rounds on Coy. Hqrs & Track at J.14.a.55.75. 6p & 11.30p. 1250 rounds at E.A.	
"	20.2.18		6p─12 (midnight) 1500 rounds on Bn Hqrs & Pioneer Dump at B.24.t.95.80. 250 950 rounds at E.A. rounds at E.A.	
"	21.2.18		9th Coy Company Relief without incident. Our M.g's fired (a) 1500 rounds on Quarry at C.25.t.85.85. (b.) 1500 rounds on J.3.8.t.70.05. (6) 1500 rounds on J.2.t.90.80. (d) 1500 rounds on R.24.t.96.80.	
"	22.2.18		2750 rounds at E.A. Battle zone reconnoitred with R.E. Commander. 1000 rounds on Quarry & Road from C.19.d.5.2 to C.25.t.94.74.	

WAR DIARY
or
INTELLIGENCE SUMMARY.
(Erase heading not required.)

Army Form C. 2118.

Place	Date	Hour	Summary of Events and Information	Remarks and references to Appendices
Trenches	23.2.18		9th 2000 rounds dumped at new positions - Battle Zone. SOS lines to cover East end of Unvillers Wood laid out for 5 rear guns of forward zone. Our MGs fired (A) 2000 rounds on Quarry, Bn HQrs at C25 c 88.80 (B) 2000 rounds on Bn HQrs & Dump at C19 a 1.8.	
	24.2.18		Our MGs fired 1000 rounds between 7 & 10 p.m. on Bn HQrs & Tracks in J.2.6.	
	25.2.18		Positions for guns in LAMBAY Switch pointed out to representative of 62nd Field Coy RE. 1100 at E.A.	
	26.2.18		Our MGs fired 1000 rounds on Dump at J.2.6. 10.99. + Bn HQrs at J.2.6. 30.30.	
	27.2.18		Teams at C.6 & C.7 changed places with teams at C.8 & C.9. 2700 rounds at E.A.	
	28.2.18		Positions in Battle Zone manned on receiving message "Battle Zone Take Precautionary measures". 2.40 p.m.	

B Humphrey / Capt
Comdg 42nd M.G. Coy

www.ingramcontent.com/pod-product-compliance
Lightning Source LLC
Chambersburg PA
CBHW081436160426
43193CB00013B/2299